MASS. IDENTITY. ARCHITECTURE.

Architectural Writings of

Jean Baudrillard

MASS. IDENTITY. ARCHITECTURE.

Architectural Writings of

Jean Baudrillard

EDITED BY

FRANCESCO PROTO

WITH A FOREWORD BY MIKE GANE
AND
AN ESSAY BY KEITH BROADFOOT AND REX BUTLER

Published in Great Britain in 2006 by Wiley-Academy,
a division of John Wiley & Sons Ltd

Copyright © 2006   John Wiley & Sons Ltd, The Atrium, Southern Gate,
Chichester, West Sussex PO19 8SQ, England
Telephone (+44) 1243 779777

First edition printed in Hardback in 2003

Email (for orders and customer service enquiries): cs-books@wiley.co.uk
Visit our Home Page on www.wileyeurope.co.uk or www.wiley.com

Other Wiley Editorial Offices

John Wiley & Sons Inc., 111 River Street, Hoboken, NJ 07030, USA

Jossey-Bass, 989 Market Street, San Francisco, CA 94103-1741, USA

Wiley-VCH Verlag GmbH, Boschstr. 12, D-69469 Weinheim, Germany

John Wiley & Sons Australia Ltd, 42 McDougall Street, Milton, Queensland
4064, Australia

John Wiley & Sons (Asia) Pte Ltd, 2 Clementi Loop #02-01,
Jin Xing Distripark, Singapore 129809

John Wiley & Sons Canada Ltd, 5353 Dundas Street West, Suite 400,
Etobicoke, Ontario M9B 6H8

ISBN-13 978 0 47002 715 8
ISBN-10 0 470 02715 0

Cover Photo & Design by Warren Dean Bonett, www.wdbonett.com

Typeset by Florence Production Ltd, UK
Printed and bound by TJ International Ltd, UK

This book is printed on acid-free paper responsibly manufactured from sustainable forestry,
in which at least three trees are planted for each one used for paper production.

CONTENTS

Foreword: **Consuming Signs**   ix

MIKE GANE

Introduction: **Philosophy as a Commodity: Mode d'Emploi**   xi

FRANCESCO PROTO

The Aesthetics and the Machine   1

FRANCESCO PROTO

Cheese-(beau)burger   Post-orgasmic chill   Pop-nography

The Prozac effect   Disneyland: one-way ticket   The emperor's new clothes

Chapter One: **Absolute Architecture**   19

The Singular Objects of Architecture

Radicality   Singular objects in architecture   Illusion. Virtuality. Reality

A destabilized area   Concept. Irresolution. Vertigo   Values of functionalism

New York or Utopia   Architecture: between nostalgia and anticipation

(Always) seduction. Provocation. Secrets   The aesthetics of modernity

A heroic architectural act?   Art, architecture and postmodernity

Visual disappointment. Intellectual disappointment   The aesthetics

of disappearance

Chapter Two: **Cool Cities**   37

America
Salt Lake City   New York   Santa Barbara   Venice and Porterville   Disneyland
The Bonaventure Hotel   The realized utopia

Cool Memories I (1980–85)
Urbino. Gubbio. Mantua   Trieste   Palermo   Pompeii   Montreal   Tower blocks
Vélizy   Vélizy 2   Versailles. St Peter   The Pompidou Centre   Urban monsters
Paris   Berlin   Rome in December   Night on the cities   Dunkirk   Ideal City
Fifth Avenue   Suburban comfort

Cool Memories II (1987–90)
American towns   Rio   Buenos Aires   Puerto Stroessner   Sites of fascination
Venice (California)   Los Angeles   Marilyn's grave   Salt Lake City. Las Vegas
Disneyworld   Beyond Las Vegas   Venice (California). New York. Lisbon
Shop windows   Shop windows 2   Arche de la Défense   Coupole   São Paulo
Copacabana

Cool Memories III (1992–95)
Venice   Puerto Vallarta   Bern. Zurich   Brasilia   Brasilia's satellites
Free zones' farce   American campuses   Pointe du Raz   Copacabana
Montreal. Rio   Pompeii   Luxembourg Gardens

Cool Memories IV (1995–2002)
New York. Tierra del Fuego   New York   Naples   Pompeii   Disney Company
Future Cities   St Petersburg   Bogotá   Buenos Aires   Palacio Itamarati
California   Villa Palagonia (Palermo)   Villa Palagonia II

Chapter Three: **The Indifference of Space**   71
Le Parc de la Villette

Urbanism and architecture

Chapter Four: **The Code and the Eye**   81
Simulations
Hyperreal and imaginary [Disneyland]   The stucco angel [Baroque Architecture]
The tactile and the digital [World Trade Center]

Trompe l'Oeil or enchanted simulation [Duke of Urbino's and Federico
da Montefeltro's studiolos]

Ecstasy and inertia [Pompeii]

Chapter Five: **The Rise of the Object: the End of Culture**   95

The Formal Liturgy of the Object

The consumer society   Profusion and display   The drugstore   Parly 2

Hypermarket and Hypercommodity

Absolute Advertising, Ground Zero Advertising

Mass (Sociology of)

Mass languages   A structure of modernity   An operational language
Beyond truth and falsehood   The internal logic of this neo-language

Chapter Six: **The Ideology of Technique**   123

Technique as social practice

The organization, as myth, of technique   Conclusion: 'technique
totally in the service of everyday life?'

Ephemeral and Durable

The Irony of Technology

The Beaubourg Effect: Implosion or Deterrence?

Chapter Seven: **The Aesthetic Suicide**   151

Questions of Strategy

Truth or Radicality: The Future of Architecture

**The Homeopathic Disappearance of Architecture:
an interview with Jean Baudrillard**   175

Aesthetics and design   The lost language of seduction   Success in
architecture   Duchamp in architecture   The object as a sign
Space as a thought

Baudrillard, Perspective and the Void of Architecture   181

KEITH BROADFOOT AND REX BUTLER

Essential Bibliography   189

Further Reading   191

Advertising in its new version is no longer the baroque, utopian scenario ecstatic over objects and consumption, but rather the effect of the omnipresent visibility of corporations, trademarks, PR men, social dialogue and the virtues of communication. With the disappearance of the public place, advertising invades everything (the street, the monument, the market, the stage, language). It determines architecture and the creation of super-objects such as Beaubourg, Les Halles or La Villette – which are literally advertising monuments (or anti-monuments) – not so much because they are centred on consumption but because from the outset these monuments were meant to be a demonstration of the operation of culture, of the cultural operation of the commodity and that of the masses in movement. Today our only architecture is just that: huge screens upon which moving atoms, particles and molecules are refracted. The public stage, the public place have been replaced by a gigantic circulation, ventilation, and ephemeral connecting space.

Jean Baudrillard, *The Ecstasy of Communication*

CONSUMING SIGNS

MIKE GANE

The most important French thinker of the past twenty years here casts his critical eye on architecture. The result is an astonishingly brilliant reading of the modern physical environment from Sydney to Paris, from Istanbul to New York, from Rio to Bangkok. Baudrillard was quick to notice the significance of the Pompidou Centre, the Bonaventure Hotel, and the World Trade Center as crucial sites of the cultural logic of modernity and postmodernity. Baudrillard's precision of observation is accompanied by an evolving philosophical position which unfailingly picks up radical indications of a new global culture. Thus this collection is not eclectic, or the simple jottings of a travelling academic. It is an essential component of one of the key intellectual trajectories of our time.

Francesco Proto has served us admirably with this selection. Certainly Baudrillard has always been interested in 'objects'. Unlike 'commodities' which carry 'exchange' value, for Baudrillard objects in the modern cultural system carry 'sign' value as well, and that is why images, logos, styles predominate today, and when they do we can be sure that we are living in a consumer society. It is Baudrillard's primary thesis that the logics of consumer societies are remarkably radical, and he has become famous as the principal theorist of this radicality, and one of the most imaginative of its opponents. He was one of the first to notice how a hypermarket can disarticulate an urban centre. Thus as can be seen in this collection his own reception of new architectural objects has hardly been uniformly celebratory. His writing on modern and postmodern culture is subtle and varied. Each encounter is reported with a freshness of experience often captured in a mode of writing, which, while critical, is also expressly poetic. But Baudrillard does not aim to produce a new aesthetic. What he writes is an analysis of the fracturing of an aesthetic, the shift towards the transaesthetic.

Theory, poetry, analysis, critique, transaesthetic. Central to the reading of this collection is the quality of Baudrillard's language and conceptual invention. Certainly Baudrillard is the author of a major contribution to the theoretical understanding of the modern world. Throughout these writings the focus is surely maintained: the experience of the world has changed, and a new terminology is thus urgently required. Baudrillard draws on new developments in art and technology with key ideas such as 'hyperreality', 'virtualisation', and so on, since one of his essential propositions is that in the modern world the whole relation with 'the real' is fundamentally altered. This change is paradoxical, for at the same time the world is reconfigured virtually, reality itself, in what Baudrillard calls a move into 'simulation', seems to have swallowed its images, its logos, so that we can no longer think of it independently from them. The world, including the practices of architecture and urban planning are not exempt. Baudrillard counterposes against this logic a complex anthropological and philosophical idea of how successful cultures work by ritual, seclusion, ceremony, seduction.

Had Baudrillard produced only a theory, however radical, it is doubtful whether he would be so widely read. The most remarkable aspect of Baudrillard's work is the way in which the writing never appears as the application of a fixed and complete theoretical dogma, but always as the playful invention of a quite new adventure. It is this quality of the poetically encountered world which is so striking. It is the direct result of his view that writing should not aim to capture the real world, but should exist as its poetic challenge. His view of a viable architecture today would, it seems, be the same. Ultimately he is one of the very few writers able to walk between conservatism and modernism with a degree of integrity.

Introduction

PHILOSOPHY AS A COMMODITY:
MODE D'EMPLOI

FRANCESCO PROTO

'One should build only those things which by their excellence
are worthy of being destroyed'.[1]

Jean Baudrillard

Maybe just a supernova at the highest point of energy emission – before
the final implosion into an unlimited gravitational mass – architecture represents
the most dazzling, and for this reason almost invisible body of evidence left by
the technological society in its attempt to get rid of reality. This exquisite corpse
– sort of Dadaist, accidental recombination – succeeded the dismemberment,
liofilization and centrifugation of culture, this singular object that we conventionally define as architecture: is *the sweet scent of decomposition*[2] starting to
affect it yet? Or, following the destiny of all of the discourses and metadiscourses
of our era – art, advertising, politics, philosophy, in other words, the redundant,
germless and sanitized counterfeit of social meaning and culture played and
showed in controlled social areas – has it already been turned into the embalmed
ghost of its own reflection?

ARCHITECTURE AS EVIDENCE.

For even the advent of post-structuralism in architecture, and the consequent attempt at dismantling the illusory coherence of its surface seems to be incapable of exceeding a melancholic faith in technology as an 'automatic' means for passive interactivity. So that the eruption of fragmentation, the aspiration to a self-destructive architectural organism, the theorization of totally incoherent systems – which led Bernard Tschumi to the sympathetic collaboration with the French philosopher Jacques Derrida for the Parc de la Villette in Paris – seems to be finally developing into the very question postmodern thought has tried to avoid: the confusion of 'surface' with 'superficial'.

Starting with a wide-ranging conversation with the French architect Jean Nouvel, in which a variety of topics is initially proposed and discussed (chapter 1), this book has been conceived as a circular pathway in which the complex entwining of issues and theoretical perspectives – following an assemblage for large thematic areas respectful of its original source – is finally revealed through the mutual relation between the unpredictable implications from different sections.

Thus, if the mimicking of road movies, which forms the basis of Baudrillard's writing strategy in *America*, has been associated with the travel-narrative of *Cool Memories* (chapter 2), the illusory game of urban utopias (Pompidou Centre, Le Parc de la Villette or the Bonaventure Hotel) – indifferent *object-cause* of towns' desertification (chapter 3) – anticipates the fatal turning of this same game into the negative universe of *Simulations* (chapter 4), where illusion is split (positive and negative illusion) and juxtaposed while ranging from large (Disneyland, Pompeii) to small (Duke of Urbino's studiolo, baroque stucco) architectural objects. In this same chapter, where the hyperreality of contemporary culture is discussed as mirrored in the hallucinogenic doubling of the World Trade Center, Baudrillard's analysis provides the presuppositions for which the 'effigy of capitalist system [. . . ,] by the grace of terrorism, [. . .] has [now] become the world's most beautiful building – the eighth wonder of the world!':

> The violence of globalization also involves architecture, and
> hence the violent protest against it also involves the
> destruction of that architecture [. . .] These architectural

monsters, like the Beaubourg Centre in Paris, have always exerted an ambiguous fascination, as have the extreme forms of modern technology – a contradictory feeling of attraction and repulsion, and hence, somewhere, a secret desire to see them disappear. In the case of the Twin Towers, something particular is added: precisely their symmetry and their twin-ness. There is, admittedly in this cloning and perfect symmetry, an aesthetic quality, a kind of perfect crime against form, a tautology of form which can give rise, in a violent reaction, to the temptation to break the symmetry, to restore an asymmetry, and hence a singularity. [. . .]

Were the Twin Towers destroyed, or did they collapse? Let us be clear about this: [. . .] the architectural object was destroyed, but it was the symbolic object which was targeted and which it was intended to demolish [. . .]

But there is more: somewhere, it was party to its own destruction. The countless disaster movies bear witness to this fantasy, which they attempt to exorcize with images and special effects. But the fascination they exert is a sign that acting-out is never far away – the rejection of any system, including internal rejection, growing all the stronger as it approaches perfection or omnipotence [. . .]

This brings us back to what should be the basic question for architecture, which architects never formulate. Is it normal to build and construct? In fact it is not, and we should preserve the absolutely problematic character of the undertaking. Undoubtedly, the task of architecture – of good architecture – is to efface itself, to disappear as such. The towers, for their part, have disappeared. But they have left us the symbol of their disappearance as symbol. They, which were the symbol of omnipotence, have become, by their absence, the symbol of the possible disappearance of that

omnipotence – which is perhaps an even more potent symbol.
Moreover, although the two towers have disappeared, they have
not been annihilated. Even in their pulverized space, they have
left behind an intense awareness of their presence. No one
who knew them can cease imagining them and the imprint
they made on the skyline from all points of the city. Their end
in material space has borne them off into a definitive
imaginary space.

Probably the least evident side of Disneyfication, the terrorist attack – in
proving the 'degeneration of the cinematographic illusion' into the catastrophic
effects of Simulation – poses itself, behind Disneyland, as 'a parody of the world
of the imagination'. If further news on the terrorists' failed attempts have in fact
revealed 'an unusual Hollywoodean scenario' (after the World Trade Center
became the protagonist of *King Kong*'s latest remake, an order was given from
Afghanistan 'to strike the [Brooklyn] bridge of Godzilla's movie'),[3] the consumption of places, in the form of mythological images, looks as if it has finally turned
architecture into a physical support of contemporary myths, a physical place for
symbolic exchange made possible by the turning of the building itself into a mega-
logo advertising its own presence and activity.

The reversal of the analysis from the consumption of places to the places
of consumption is thus set out in chapter 5, where hypermarkets, hypercom-
modities, advertising and the desire of the masses for culture as a fatal instrument
of self-attributed identity comes to the fore. In this respect, if chapter 6 provides
a survey of late/post-modernist conceptual overturning and misinterpretation of
modernist principles of progress and technique, in chapter 7 de-materialization is
identified as the possible achievement, by architecture, to recover those characteristics of challenging complicity that everywhere, and anyway, seduction has lost
in the maze of diffused and disarticulated *jouissance*.

The final interview, and the following essay by Broadfoot and Butler,
which close the book, represent and suggest, a possible, personal interpretation of
a body of work whose devastating time-bomb effect in architecture is yet to come.

Notes

1. Jean Baudrillard, *The Spirit of The Machine*, 2003, London: Verso, p. 6.
2. This expression has been borrowed from Zygmunt Bauman's essay in Chris Rojek and Bryan S Turner (eds), *Forget Baudrillard?*, 1993, London: Routledge, p 22.
3. 'Bin Laden was inspired by Cinema', *Il Messaggero*, 16 June 2003, p 15.

THE AESTHETICS AND THE MACHINE

FRANCESCO PROTO

Cheese-(beau)burger

When Renzo Piano and Richard Rogers completed the Pompidou Centre in Paris no one knew, and they themselves could hardly have imagined, that this anti-monument to culture would contribute to the sudden overturning of the concept of contemporary architecture masking it behind the merciless superficiality of the form: the image.

Image is everything (and vice-versa): in its escape from both nature and death, the Apollonian Western eye seems to have come to an extreme compromise. Aestheticising reality into its own simulacrum, the regime of vision has in fact accelerated the process of flattening reality to the point of entirely annihilating the distance of the gaze.[1] We are *in* what we see, we are *what* we see. Merged in the domain of the scopic drive, images supply a new ontology of self-apprehension and objectification of identity.

Excess of consumption, speed of assumption (the *ictu oculi* and the optical device): from the abyss of late modern capitalism, what is consumed is not the object anymore, but the solipsistic relationship with the object.

> What's great about this country [Andy Warhol confided to his
> diary] is that America started the tradition where the richest
> consumers buy essentially the same things as the poorest. You
> can be watching TV and see Coca-Cola, and you can know
> that the President drinks Coke, Liz Taylor drinks Coke, and
> just think, you can drink Coke, too . . . When Queen Elizabeth
> came here and President Eisenhower bought her a hot dog I'm
> sure that . . . [n]ot for a dollar, not for ten dollars, not for a
> hundred thousand dollars could she get a better hot dog. She
> could get one for twenty cents and so could anybody else.[2]

That is what the Pompidou Centre represented when it was built, and still
represents after 25 years and more than one hundred and fifty million visitors: a
media-saturated simulation in charge of exhausting the stereotypes of cultural
degradation. Eventually, the loss of its most thrilling feature – an immense electronic billboard façade for the joyful and cacophonic dissemination of visual
messages – for the fear of uncontrolled political manipulation – turned the building
from a symbol of democratic civilization into a parody of ideological gratification. As a Lacanian *Point de Capiton*, this simple detail betrayed the euphoric
spontaneity of the May Events and instituzionalized the unfocused complaints of
the previous decade into a monument to entertainment and display.

Beabourg-parking, Beabourg-institute for advanced studies in music
and acoustic (IRCAM). Beabourg-library, museum and children's workshop.
Beaubourg-auditorium, Beaubourg-restaurant, Beaubourg-bar and industrial
design center. Beaubourg-piazza, theatre and hall. Indeed, BEAUBOURG-
MACHINE. Unsurprisingly meant to duplicate the iconic *esprit* of Oscar
Nitzchke's Maison de la Publicité, the Pompidou truly grazed the cybernetic
adaptation of the *decorated shed*. The conceptual apotheosis of post-modern games
– an independent and flat plane for the random application of decoration – the
latter did not match masses' aspiration to social status (while the Pompidou's
monumentalism reabsorbed elitism as a surplus-value).

The Pompidou's violation of the postmodern codes – the implosion of
mass-cultured signs' overdose into the solitary sign of the escalator as a mega-

REDUCED TO URGENT IMAGE

logo – will end up generating the invasion of architectural icons and, therefore, the unconditional celebration, during the 80s, of Philip Johnson's AT&T Building. Among these super-advertising logos – the collapse of the building into a peremptory image – the Pompidou Centre stood as the deconsecrated founder of the family line, the death rattle of the one-eyed post-modern wave that will leave behind it a massacre already foreseen by the *International Situationist*: the extermination of art, culture, advertising and the social; and finally, by the latter, the extinction of architecture through euthanasia. Its corpse will rise again twenty years later, but only in the singular fabric of its own reflection.

AT&T Building

The advent of kitsch in architecture, which reached a very intellectualised profile during the first half of the 1980s, gave birth to a series of highly stylised buildings in which historical matrices – such as Philip Johnson's AT&T Chippendale profile – fused and flattened into the design scheme, become iconically denotative.

Photo credit: © Tony and Peter Mackertich

Post orgasmic-chill

Like Warhol's *Campbell's Soup Can* – the objectification of consumption through the objects' dissipation – the Pompidou too represents both the end of social architecture and the implosion of the social into architecture. However, interpreting the Pompidou as a (cultural) supermarket is as inadequate as defining a (proper) supermarket as a museum. It is precisely the tangible dimension of possession that at the Pompidou is missing, exchanged as it is for the social operation of culture adulteration.

> There lies the supreme irony of Beaubourg: the masses throw
> themselves at it, not because they salivate for that culture
> which they have been denied for centuries, but because they
> have for the first time the opportunity to massively participate
> in this great mourning of a culture that, in the end, they have

> always detested . . . The masses rush toward Beaubourg as they
> rush toward disaster sites, with the same irresistible élan.
> Better: they are the disaster of Beaubourg . . . Not only does
> their weight put the building in danger, but their adhesion,
> their curiosity annihilates the very contents of this culture of
> animation.[3]

The importance of the Pompidou is thus ascribed not only to the disappearance of the symbol in favour of the sign, but also to the definitive entrance
of history into the n-powered aesthetic dimension, the stage where the meta-narra-
tive 'democracy of free time'[4] is performed, mirrored and doubled.

> What should, then, have been placed in Beaubourg? Nothing.
> The void that would have signified the disappearance of any
> culture of meaning and aesthetic sentiment [. . .] Culture is a
> site of the secret, of seduction, of initiation, of a restrained and
> highly ritualized symbolic exchange.[5]

More precisely, it is art that, in losing the initial polemic spirit of
the avant-garde, takes up a position between surprise and reassurance – art is
everywhere, the irrevocable restyling of commodities when everything has already
been restyled. Here lies its strength: conclusive transparency of content, then no
content at all, but a pure fascination for something whose existence can only
be verified.

The Pop Art Movement investigated advertising mechanisms. It took them
to pieces, dissected them and finally reassembled them. It developed them –
absorbing the sublime into the subliminal – and returned them to the sender. The
assumption by the work of art of all of the distinctive features of commodities
(reproducibility in return for the *aura*) thus amounted to a pure feedback-effect
by the means of which commodities themselves ended up in assuming all of the
distinctive features of art. The beautiful expired, but pleasantness has survived in
the guise of taste and market demand.

Reasonably doomed to manifest what commodities lean towards – the vanishing point of meaning, its absolute unreasonableness – the *Campbell's Soup Can* is a dialogue with no interlocutors, a test that does not admit of replies. Flat, cool, meaningless but nevertheless agreeable, familiar, reproducible. Democratic. The *Campbell's Soup Can* proposes itself already consumed by both memory and the gaze – a pure sign behind which the original emerges only as an analogy. The technique that Warhol employed to reiterate its reproduction – serigraphy – charges the can of a hunky-dory flavour of corroded smoothness that operates a metaphorization of ready-made visual appropriation. Semiotics proclaims surprise to be an unexpected feature meant to enhance communication. Nothing to do with a cool and idle attraction meant to flatten ineffective information: depth, light, thickness – emotion. The last of art's special effect, the *Campbell's Soup Can* is a metalinguistic vortex indifferent to its content – the proliferation of images in the watertight containers of un-biodegradable aestheticisation.

'What are you doing after the orgy?' a businessman therefore asks one of his lovers on board his private jet. A rule rather than an exception, this scene from an Hollywoodian film densifies the post-orgasmic chill we are left with after too fast a rupture with a system in which '[. . .] everything has become sexual, everything is subjected to desire: power, knowledge, everything is interpreted in terms of phantom and removal [. . .] And contemporarily everything aestheticises itself: politics aestheticises itself into the spectacle, sex into publicity and pornography, the whole gamut of activities into what is held to be called culture [. . .] a sort of mediatic and media semiologising process which invades everything – THE XEROX DEGREE OF CULTURE.'[6]

Pop-nography

The legendary fantasy of a saga in which individuals become spectators of their own lives: 'In this world of the Kodak camera, of *Paris-Match* magazine', Neil Leach states, 'people can only perceive themselves as though they are being captured on celluloid or featured on the glossy pages of a glamorous magazine.'[7]

IT'S REAL

The front cover of *It's Real*, a magazine in which the entire life of an nonexistent rock star (Joanna Zychowicz) is compressed into a few pages. The excess of details about Joanna's 'scandalous' life – provided by false 'scoops' – gives a realistic background to the mechanics of advertising on the one hand, and on the other establishes a silent and self-aware complicity with the consumer, where the sarcastic use of the medium finally substitutes itself for the product.

Photos courtesy of *It's Real* magazine

If in the advertising campaign for Diesel jeans – 'the luxury of dirt' – the identity of the consumer is sublimated in the 'dirt' of clothes, through the use of specific colourings these are made to appear greasy, it is in *It's Real* magazine that the dirt of commodities is sold in its double meaning of both gimmick and 'aura' – a trade-off between the vulgar and shameless life of the Polish rock star Joanna Zychowicz and that of an ordinary individual furnished, through a simple bill of sale, with the opportunity to ascend to an existential simulacrum.[8] As near as is possible to realising the myth of the superequipped Barbie, the luxury of dirt is capable of moulding a spectator for whom it acts as the stylised stigmata of a life deprived of the meaning of experience; and, as with the Dolby Surround effect in the cinema, it contributes to dragging him/her into the trance of identification.

This scenographic surplus, applied to the fabric of jeans – a sort of footprint on the holy shroud – is pornography in panavision on the screens of our imagination, a total, unveiled exhibition of an embrace between the spectator and his/her double. A media invention created by the advertising market, Joanna Zychowicz does not, in fact, exist . . . but only until there is proof to the contrary – a proof that we ourselves give. Joanna is us and our need to be her; she is the reassurance of an existence that belongs to us by right. Joanna is the show in which we are waiting to perform, the chance we cannot miss, the testimonial of our presence – a sort of vital self-certification.

Ritualised among the stereotypes of consumption where the product, as well as the consumer, exists only as a projection, the 'luxury of dirt' represents the end of irony and the beginning of a new innocence (Codeluppi), the legitimisation of a narrative meta-genre in which obscenity is nevermore configured as the aestheticisation of the disappearance of seduction, but as the aestheticisation of its final putrefaction.

The Prozac effect

Guarantor for the existence of a mass unrooted from the hateful obviousness of the social conflict, the Pompidou Centre has the enviable primacy of having broken, once and for ever, the rationalist anguish affecting modernism.

The fact that the distributive system (role) of the building never really worked, especially after the latest restoration which has made it totally inflexible, means that no one has ever been concerned about the centre's supposed functionalism, apart from those militant critics threatened by its symptomatic deflagration.

The shift of function onto an *allegorical* fiction epitomized in fact a shift in functional presuppositions, from technological flexibility as a product for the consumption of democracy to democracy as a flexible by-product of consumption.

The building's assembly-kit effect, which reworked in a High-Tech style the megastructural model of the previous decade, greatly contributed to suggesting the do-it-yourself dimension of contemporary culture. As a fairground attraction, a petroleum refinery, an astonishing supertanker unpredictably stranded in the middle of Paris (Duchamp's old trick of Dadaist decontextualization) suddenly metamorphosed into an architectural counterfeit; the structure, which appeared to be a technological prodigy, the highest expression of both prefabrication and standardisation, had indeed dried up the initial budget for transportation and the handmade production of the single elements.

POMPIDOU CENTRE

Through the impudent transparency of its facade, the Beaubourg represents the annihilation of the semiotic relationship (signifier/signified) between the building and the facade itself. It is not by accident that the collapsing of the latter into the graphic sign of the escalator coincides perfectly with the logo for the products sold in the museum shop.

Photo credit: © Martin Charles

Nevertheless, through its mobile floors and its self-moving walls, it eventually realised the ideal of a work-in-progress structure, in which lightness and transformability would increase the users' involvement. That is, in acting as an interactive object – the Pompidou Centre also anticipated the advertising system's new frontiers which, transplanted onto the Net, provide the unexpected opportunity to alter the message from the inside. Hence, the myth of a commodity that, in looking capable of simultaneously working as both an advertisement and a product, transfers manipulation – unceasingly pillaging illusions when faced with the incredibility that nothing is interposed between desire and its satisfaction.

By enacting the 'maternal' and 'regressive' function peculiar to publicity (information messages have not a decisive effect on the consumer, who is nevertheless sensitive to the latent issue of protection and gratification; Codeluppi), this sacred cow of democracy – Big (m)Other spreading knowledge in a liberal emanation of equality – offered the opportunity of an incest prompted by the enormous, transparent facade, which still exhorts violation of its content. An invitation to a collective rape: the building exposes its hymen to be rent to the bitter end – and, to the bitter end, to be regenerated in the instantaneity of the Event.

This enormous glass facade, a geni(t)al example of styling accomplished by commodities and showing, in its whole, an eventually reassuring uterus, finally annihilates the castration complex of a mass indifferent to platonic love –

a propaganda operation that celebrates the Oedipus relationship distanced from guilt.

Freed from centuries of frigidity, in the Pompidou culture finally becomes a typical example of transvestitism in which the particular characteristics of the original gender, once frustrated, are emancipated, made visible and therefore unambiguous. For even these characteristics, though stated with exaggeration, makes it clear that the relationship is a paying one and, most of all, one without repercussions.

Truly visible in the darkness of time, bartering the rapture of discovery for the hysteria of possession, this enormous architectural billboard has finally realised the dream of commodities: a self-representing and self-celebrating simulacrum, a supersign in which the Renaissance illusion of space is annihilated into the everyday-space of illusion.

The Pompidou Centre and the culture it should have stood for, represents a cheeseburger served during a Buckingham Palace banquet: maybe bigger, maybe larger, with sesame seeds and cashew nuts, but so insipid as to arouse in us the desire to bite it again.

Disneyland: one-way ticket

The experience of one's double, as authentic as one's need to resemble it, is the presupposition which the success of Walt Disney's theme parks is based on. Millions of people go there to interface, and thus appropriate, the autocratic showcase of western middle-class taste. Reinterpreted in popular form, even stripped of any ironic asides, the entire postmodern experience re-emerges in Epcot or Eurodisney, where the democracy of consumption matches the democracy of taste for an immediate impact that hits below the belt.

Morris Lapidus, the creator of the Fontainebleau Hotel in Miami, which was made famous by the James Bond film *Goldfinger*, illustrates with extreme cynicism how the building, rather than being an extravagant caprice of the client, answers to precise market demands:

> Some people demand the stage setting. They want background
> . . . just as the people in Seagram's achieved status because
> they sat against this impeccable historic background which no
> one could question . . . When I started the Fontainebleau Hotel
> . . . I drew the first sketches, and the owner said, 'You must be
> crazy. I don't want this. I want French Provincial.' . . . So I
> took out some pictures of French Provincial, and I said, 'Is this
> what you want?' He said, 'Oh, my God, not that old-fashioned
> French Provincial.' [So] I . . . tr[ied] to create a sense of
> opulence and excitement and 'French provincial.' . . . I gave
> him his French, which is not French. I gave him fluted
> columns which are not contemporary. They are not French.
> I showed him a picture and I said, 'Now, look at this. It's a
> French column, this old-fashioned column. Do you want it?'
> 'Oh, no, no, no.' I showed him my fluted columns. 'Now
> you're catching the spirit,' he said.[9]

Maybe the first example of a daydream-shaped town, Celebration[10] was built according to the Average American Taste. In combining the Greek Revival, the Regency Style and the Colonial, this eclectic pastiche is an ever present stage set that stays on after the television is turned off.

The muddy monster minded to vindicate Celebration's attractions – an aberration from the *X-Files* TV series – is an allegory of the fragility of both dreamscapes and the phagocytosis of ideal scenarios.

The internalization of tourist guides and television programmes, the replacement of direct experience in the very moment of verification – if reality is not up to the fantasia cultivated in the imagination – enables representation to superimpose on presentation.

In between old-fashionable nostalgia and supermarket familiarity, at Disneyland an infinitely greater number of adults than children experience the feeling of obsolescence that Warhol first performed in his works: a subliminal

sensation of déjà-vu that allows 'as at the Museum of Modern Art in New York
... to ascertain at which point the originals resemble the copies'.[11]

On the other side of the Atlantic what is consumed is therefore the jouissance of recognizing: at Disneyland Paris thousands of American families absolve
the divine right of 'coming home' staring at the metastasis of their own (imaginary) world. Mostly, they enjoy reassurance, and tired of the unknown vortex of
the *calli*, crowd into McDonald's a few metres from piazza San Marco, to later
hypostatize Venice from the inner side of the mirror.

The consumption of déjà-vu, the announced spectacle, eventually illustrates that the experience of Disneyland is mostly intended for adults, whose
appetite for distraction is assigned some sense only when framed by a staging
kind of 'induction'. It is a question of identity.

'One goes to Disneyland to demonstrate that s/he has been there, and
thus provide the proof. It is a sightseeing to the future perfect that finds its
reasons later, when one shows to relatives and friends, commenting on them, the
photographs that the child took of his/her father while he was filming him/her,
then his/her father's film, as a crossed-proof.'[12]

Subjected to the fragmentation between reality and simulation and using
children as a pretext, everyone in Disneyland tries, like the replicants in *Blade
Runner*, to testify to a present that is already past. The impossibility of tracing a
clear line between human and artificial beings makes the totalising power of simulacra evident: in an unreal situation, the borderline between the true and the
counterfeit disappears. Replicants do not have a true history, but they can build
one since history, for everybody, has been reduced to the proof represented by a
photograph (Harvey):

> We live in an age that puts history on stage, which makes a
> spectacle of it and, in this respect, de-realises reality – whether
> this reality is the Gulf War, the castles of the Loire or the
> Niagara Falls. This distantiation, this spectacularisation is
> never as apparent as it is in travel advertisements suggesting
> tours, a series of 'instant' visions that will reach the maximum

of reality only when we will see them 'again' on the slides
through which we will impose the vision-exegesis on a
resigned audience of relatives and friends. At Disneyland, it is
the spectacle itself that is spectacularised: the scene reproduces
what was already stage and fiction – either Pinocchio's house
or *Star Wars*' starship. Inverting Woody Allen's *The Purple
Rose of Cairo*, not only do we enter the screen, but we also
discover that behind the screen there is only another screen.

The journey to Disneyland thus results in being a
second-powered tourism, the quintessence of tourism: what we
go and see does not exist. There we experience a pure liberty,
with no aim, no reason, nothing at stake. We find there neither
America nor our childhood, but the absolute arbitrariness of a
game of images which each of those who is near to us, and
that we will never see anymore, can put into whatever s/he
likes. Disneyland is today's world, in what it has as both its
best and its worst: the experience of emptiness and liberty.[13]

The emperor's new clothes

The entrance on stage of the Pompidou-object (the object's reverberating
fascination as a tactile hallucination) and the manifestation of masses as a variable in the architectural equation, finally certify the defeat of programmatic
functionality.

With the disappearance of the public place, advertising invades
everything (the street, the monument, the market, the stage,
language). It determines architecture and the creation of super-
objects such as Beaubourg, Les Halles or La Villette which are
literally advertising monuments (or anti-monuments), not so
much because they are centred on consumption but because,
from the outset, these monuments were meant to be a

demonstration of the operation of culture, of the cultural operation of the commodity and that of the masses in movement. Today our only architecture is just that: huge screens upon which moving atoms, particles and molecules are refracted. The public stage, the public place have been replaced by a gigantic circulation, ventilation and ephemeral connecting space.[14]

From this point of view, Gehry's Guggenheim Museum in Bilbao assumes the dimension of the best marketing process from the Pompidou Centre's age. It is an innovative and incandescent product in the spectacular performance of its titanium covering, whose piercing through hyperreal from the virtual (the structure has been completely computer-generated) has furnished this Never-ending Immaterial Event with the most beautiful and iridescent wrapping paper in architectural history.

For this reason, the Guggenheim Museum, like the Pompidou Centre, prospers in the myth of a gift the cultural potlatch and the nature of its myth as a *fait accompli*.

In contrast to the Guggenheim Museum, where Gehry exploited the opportunity it offered to propose a 'rewrapped' object, the impossible-to-repeat shock of the Pompidou was caused by the fact that, once and for ever, the building was offered 'unwrapped'.

In antithesis to the tacit rules of postmodern fiction, the entire symbolism of the Pompidou facade – rather than acting as a kind of self-conscious deceit in order to mediate the desire for the object – disappeared in the transparency of the facade. Postmodernism knew very well that all gifts

GUGGENHEIM MUSEUM
Though opposed to its principle, the Bauhaus diffused the perfect integration between aesthetic and function in the industrial product. In the Guggenheim Museum in Bilbao, the boundaries between architecture and design become more indistinguishable than ever before.

Photo credit: © Tony and Peter Mackertich.

must be intentionally declared, since every well-wrapped article is an illusory covering that, keeping its distance from the naked violence of desire, preserves the identity of the content[15]. (From this point of view, Venturi's 'decorated shed' is a lesson in good manners.)

Subverting this rule, the Pompidou enacted a nonrepeating operation that, similar to the conceptual significance of the Dadaist ready-made, allowed Gehry the return to the orthodoxy of the canon. Unpreserved and lacking in defences the cultural offering in Paris became an acquired right. When the building was built, Postmodernism had already lost its disrupting dialogue between signs, since advertisements, which had already invaded everything, made their drastic reduction necessary. The entire structure therefore collapsed in the supergraphic sign of the escalator, which reduced the facade to a neutral background.

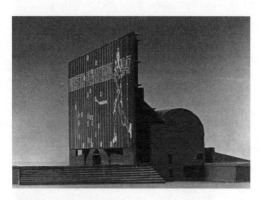

DECORATED SHED
Inspired by the complexity of Las Vegas casinos' signs, Venturi's decorated shed represents a fundamental step towards the bidimensionalization of the architectural structure, which loses the space-time dimension to conform to the faster and faster rhythms of information. Part of Venturi's analysis on the strip, in *Learning from Las Vegas*, was in fact focused on visual messages being able to impose themselves on the observer's attention at an average speed of 60 kilometres an hour.

Photo credit: © Venturi, Scott Brown and Associates

The Pompidou Centre is Salome who, in the excited frenzy of the dance, asks for the head of contemporary art. The facadeless Pompidou is the *sparagmòs* of knowledge caused by a mass enraged by the horror of the decapitation once the craving for this had been satisfied.

The transparency of the building thus represents the pure violence of a desire that claims immediate satisfaction. A satisfaction that, in the end, turns into the elimination of this same desire. It will take almost twenty years for architecture to oppose its destiny.

If the success of the Guggenheim is to be attributed to the feedbacking shock of an unusual wrapping paper, the success of Jean Nouvel's Cartier Foundation in Paris, where the content definitively renounces its container, depends upon the presence of the only covering: a holographic surface that, with nothing to wrap, leans on the inertia of refractions.

The Cartier Foundation therefore opposes the stupefaction of emptiness with the temptation of light, the seduction of transparency, the seven veils dancing out from the body of Salome: beyond the surface of illusion there is the illusion of a surface that, in its limpidity, makes a fool of thought's obtuseness.

In the Institute of the Arab World in Paris, Nouvel had already succeeded in escaping the pornography of the gaze; and by not obstructing the vision of the building from the outside, but protecting the visitor from the vision of the new town from the inside. This same facade, categorically opaque in the Institute, to negate the presence of the volume to the gaze, and opalescent in the Cartier Foundation, exhibits the body of evidence: the trace left by the image in its successful attempt to free itself from the object. A sort of tautological revenge on the invading materialism of the form, here abstraction succeeds the paralysis of meaning caused by commodities, exactly as commodities had succeeded the allegorical power of art.

In doing this, the Cartier Foundation gives shape to a different category of appearance which, in the instant reading of the visual message, substitutes its figurative simulacrum not only for the identity of

FONDATION CARTIER+Arab World Institute
Venturi's super advertising sign, which in the Beaubourg turns itself into an enormous, multipurpose display, ends up being completely transparent in the Fondation Cartier – the redundancy of messages in the information society has made these same messages useless because they are unassimilable.

Photo credits: © Philippe Ruault

matter – that is, the pure image – but also for the spectacle of the image itself. A spectacle that acts for the complete annihilation of communication – the supreme form of linguistic democracy.

With no information except for the purely sensorial – the game of refractions, which modify perception according to the quality, quantity and displacement of light, and also change according to the position assumed by the observer in relation to the building or to specific climatic conditions during both day and night – the Cartier Foundation makes itself the mouthpiece of a new dialectic capable of reinstating the lost relationship between the individual and the object.

This is not irony, but a gamble: Nouvel has interwoven the emperor's new clothes with reflexes. And, if the spell is not to be irremediably broken, it would be better if no one pointed out that the emperor is naked.

Notes

1.   Here distance means a critical distance from the object, an awareness (by the eye) of the object itself.

2.   Andy Warhol, *The Philosophy of Andy Warhol: from A to B and back again*, London: Harcourt Brace Jovanovich, 1975, pp 100–1.

3.   Jean Baudrillard, 'The Beaubourg Effect: implosion or deterrence?' in *Simulacra and Simulation*, Ann Arbor: University of Michigan Press, 1994, p 65.

4.   The word free-time itself 'ideologically' suggests that time is a democratic subject. Apparently, no one has to pay for it. Precisely because of its name, free-time appears free, even though the fact that it is the result of a subtraction from working-time makes it liable to be economically exchanged. In advertising terms, it might be: 'Sell time, buy culture.' What should seem tautologically democratic is, at this point, money itself.

5.   Baudrillard, 'The Beaubourg Effect', p 114–15.

6.   Jean Baudrillard, 'Transpolitics, Transexuality, Transaesthetics,' in William Stearns and William Chaloupka (eds), *Jean Baudrillard: the disappearance of art and politics*, trans Michel Valentin, London: Macmillan, 1992, p 10.

7.   Neil Leach, *The Anaesthetics of Architecture*, London: MIT Press, 1999, p 57.

8.   The campaign, which started in spring 2000, has now developed into the subtler, ironic and almost poetic pay-off: 'Happiness/Pleasure/Freedom is now sponsored by Diesel.'

9.   John W Cook and Heinrich Klotz (eds), *Conversations with Architects*, foreword Vincent Scully, New York/Washington: Praeger Publishers, 1973, pp 173–6.

10.   Celebration (Florida, Disney Development Company) was founded in 1994 on Disney-owned land. Developed by Robert AM Stern architects and Cooper Robertson partners, the masterplan moved from Walt Disney's original vision for Epcot mainly based on modernism and futurism to the concept of 'new urbanism' to emphasise parks, sidewalks and a mix of both commercial and residential space. Public and major buildings were designed by renowned architects like Venturi & Scott Brown Associates (Bank), Philip Johnson (Town Hall), Michael Graves (Post Office), Cesar Pelli (Cinema) and Aldo Rossi (Office Pack).

11.   Marc Augé, 'Un etnologo a Disneyland' in *Disneyland e Altri non-luoghi*, trans Francesco Proto, Turin: Bollati Boringhieri, pp 18–19.

12.   Ibid, pp 19–20.

13.   Ibid, pp 24–5.

14.   Jean Baudrillard, *The Ecstasy of Communication*, ed Sylvère Lotringer, trans Bernard and Caroline Schutze, New York: Semiotext(e), 1987, pp 19–20.

15.   Bazon Brock, 'La confezione salva i desideri contro il contagio della purezza e dell' 'identita', *Domus* n 790, February 1997.

Chapter One

ABSOLUTE ARCHITECTURE

The Singular Objects of Architecture[1]

Radicality

Jean Baudrillard: We can't begin with nothing because, logically, nothingness is the culmination of something. When I think of radicality, I think of it more in terms of writing and theory than of architecture. I am more interested in the radicality of space ... But it's possible that true radicality is the radicality of nothingness. Is there a radical space that is also a void? The question interests me because now, at last, I have an opportunity to gain insight into how we can fill a space, how we can organize it by focusing on something other than its radical extension – vertically or horizontally, that is – within a dimension where anything is possible. Yet we still need to produce something real ... The question I want to ask Jean Nouvel, since we have to start somewhere, is very simple: 'Is there such a thing as architectural truth?'

Jean Nouvel: What do you mean by 'truth'?

JB: Architectural truth isn't a truth or a reality in the sense that architecture might exhaust itself in its references, its finalities, its destination, its modes, its procedures. Doesn't architecture transcend all of that, effectively exhausting itself in something else, its true finality, or something that would enable it to go beyond its true finality ... Does architecture exist beyond this limit of the real?

Singular objects in architecture

JB: I've never been interested in architecture. I have no specific feelings about it one way or the other. I'm interested in space, yes, and in anything in so-called 'constructed' objects that enables me to experience the instability of space. I'm most interested in buildings like Beaubourg, the World Trade Center, Biosphere 2 – singular objects, but objects that aren't exactly architectural wonders as far as I'm concerned. It's not the architectural sense of these buildings that captivates me but the world they translate. If I examine the truth of the twin towers of the World Trade Center, for example, I see that, in that location, architecture expresses, signifies, translates a kind of full, constructed form, the context of a society already experiencing hyperrealism. Those two towers resemble two perforated bands. Today we'd probably say they're clones of each other, that they've already been cloned. Did they anticipate our present? Does that mean that architecture is not part of reality but part of the fiction of a society, an anticipatory illusion? Or does architecture simply translate what is already there? That's why I asked, 'Is there such a thing as architectural truth?' in the sense that there would be a suprasensible destination for architecture and for space.

JN: ... If we attempt to talk about architecture as a limit – and that's what really interests me – we do so by always positioning ourselves on the fringe of knowledge and ignorance. That's the true adventure of architecture. And that adventure is situated in a real world, a world that implies a consensus. You said, somewhere, that a consensus must exist in order for seduction to occur. Now, the field of architecture is a field that, by the very nature of things, revolves around a world of seduction. The architect is in a unique situation. He's not an artist in the traditional sense. He's not someone who meditates in front of a blank page. He doesn't work on a canvas. I often compare the architect to the film director, because we have roughly the same limitation ...

In my case, I've looked for it in the articulation of various things, especially the formulation of a certain way of thinking. So should I use the word 'concept' or not? I used it very early on, realizing that the word is philosophically appropriate. Then we may want to introduce the terms 'percept' and 'affect' in reference to Deleuze, but that's not the real problem. The problem lies in our ability to articulate a project around a preliminary concept or idea, using a very specific strategy that can synergize – or sometimes even juxtapose – perceptions that will interact with one another and define a place we are unfamiliar with. We are still dealing with invention, the unknown, risk. This unfamiliar place, if we succeed in figuring out what's going on, could be the locus of a secret. And it might, assuming that's the case, then convey certain things, things we cannot control, things that are fatal, voluntarily uncontrolled. We need to find a compromise between what we control and what we provoke. All the buildings I've tried to build until now are based on the articulation of these three things. They also refer to a concept that I know interests you, the concept of illusion.

Illusion. Virtuality. Reality

JN: I'm no magician, but I try to create a space that isn't legible, a space that works as the mental extension of sight. This seductive space, this virtual space of illusion is based on very precise strategies, strategies that are often diversionary. I frequently use what I find around me, including . . . cinema. So when I say that I play with depth of field, it's because I'm trying to foreground a series of filters that could lead anywhere – a kind of metanarrative but from that point on, the intellect goes into action. This is not entirely my invention. Look at the Japanese garden. There is always a vanishing point, the point at which we don't know whether the garden stops or continues. I'm trying to provoke that sort of response.

If we look at the phenomenon of perspective – I'm thinking of the project for superimposing a grid on the horizon, which I had prepared for La Tête Défense – I was attempting to step outside Alberti's logic. In other words, I was trying to organize all the elements in such a way that they could be read in series and, if need be, to play with scale using the series' rhythm, so the viewer would become conscious of the space. What happens if I escape those limits? What if I say that the building isn't between the horizon and the observer but is part of that horizon? Assuming this, what happens if it loses its materiality?

Dematerialization is something that would interest you; the 'endless skyscraper' is one example. [Nouvel's project for a *tour sans fin*, or 'endless skyscraper', was designed for La Défense, just outside central Paris. Although his design won an international competition, the building was never constructed.] Again, this isn't something I invented. I think Deleuze, in *Proust and Signs*, spoke about it from a different point of view. This diversion, which reroutes our perception of phenomena from the material to the immaterial, is a concept that architecture should appropriate for itself. Using these kinds of concepts, we can create more than what we see. And this 'more than what we see' is manifest in and through physical context. With respect to what architecture has borrowed from cinema, the concept of sequence is very important as Paul Virilio reminds us. In other words, concepts such as displacement, speed, memory seen in terms of an imposed trajectory, or a known trajectory, enable us to compose an architectural space based not only on what we see but on what we have memorized as a succession of sequences that are perceived to follow one another. From this point on, there are contrasts between what is created and what was originally present in our perception of space . . .

[Thus] when I play with the concept of a virtual space, in the magician's sense, it's because space and architecture are things we become conscious of through our eyes. So we can play with anything the eye can integrate through sight, and we can fool the eye. Classical culture has often made use of this kind of sleight of hand. In a building like the Cartier Foundation, where I intentionally blend the real image and the virtual image, it signifies that within a given plane, I no longer know if I'm looking at the virtual image or the real image . . . These are gimmicks, things we can put into our bag of tricks, our architectural bag of tricks, and which we're never supposed to talk about, but which, from time to time, must be talked about. These are the means by which architecture creates a virtual space or a mental space; it's a way of tricking the senses. But it's primarily a way of preserving a destabilized area.

A destabilized area

[. . .]

JB: I agree, except perhaps about terms like 'consensus.' When you say that seduction is consensual, I'm sceptical.

JN: You mean only with reference to architecture?

JB: Precisely. It's a way of confronting it through the visible and the invisible . . . What I like very much in your work is that we don't see it, things remain invisible, they know how to make themselves invisible. When you stand in front of the buildings, you see them, but they're invisible to the extent that they effectively counteract that hegemonic visibility, the visibility that dominates us, the visibility of the system, where everything must be immediately visible and immediately interpretable. You conceive space in such a way that architecture simultaneously creates both place and nonplace, is also a nonplace in this sense, and thus creates a kind of apparition. And it's a seductive space. So I take back what I said earlier: seduction isn't consensual. It's dual. It must confront an object with the order of the real, the visible order that surrounds it. If this duality doesn't exist – if there's no interactivity, no context – seduction doesn't take place. A successful object, in the sense that it exists outside its own reality, is an object that creates a dualistic relation, a relation that can emerge through diversion, contradiction, destabilization, but which effectively brings the so-called reality of a world and its radical illusion face-to-face.

Concept. Irresolution. Vertigo

JB: Let's talk about radicality. Let's talk about the kind of radical exoticism of things that Ségalen discusses, the estrangement from a sense of identity that results in the creation of a form of vertigo through which all sorts of things can occur: affects, concepts, prospects, whatever, but always something insoluble, something unresolved. In this sense, yes, architectural objects, or at least yours or others that are even more undomesticated, are part of an architecture without a referent. This reflects their quality of being 'unidentified,' and ultimately unidentifiable, objects. This is one area where we can combine – and not merely by deliberate analogy – writing, fiction, architecture, and a number of other things as well, obviously, whether this involves the analysis of a society, an event, or an urban context. I agree that we can't choose the event, we can only choose the concept, but we retain the right to make this choice. The choice of a concept is something that should conflict with the context, with all the significations (positive, functional, etc.) a building can assume, or a theory, or anything else.

Deleuze defined the concept as something antagonistic. However, with respect to the event, as it is given, as it is seen, as it is deciphered, overdetermined by the media or other voices, by information, the concept is that which creates the nonevent. It creates an event to the extent that it juxtaposes the so-called 'real' event with a theoretical or fictional nonevent of some sort. I can see how this can happen with writing, but I have a much harder time with architecture. In your work, I feel it in the effect produced by this illusion you spoke of earlier; not in the sense of an illusion or a *trompe l'oeil* – well, ultimately, yes, of course, but not an illusion in the sense of a simulation – of something that takes place beyond the reflection of things or beyond the screen. Today we are surrounded by screens. In fact, it's rare to succeed in creating a surface or place that doesn't serve as a screen and can exert all the prestige of transparency without the dictatorship.

I'd like to make a distinction here regarding our terminology. Illusion is not the same as the virtual, which, in my opinion, is complicit with hyperreality, that is, the visibility of an imposed transparency, the space of the screen, mental space, and so on. Illusion serves as a sign for anything else. It seems to me that everything you do, and do well, is another architecture seen through a screen. Precisely because to create something like an inverse universe, you must completely destroy that sense of fullness, that sense of ripe visibility, that over-signification we impose on things.

And here I'd like to know, as part of this question of context, what happens to social and political data, to everything that can constrain things, when architecture is tempted to become the expression, or even the sociological or political transformer, of a social reality, which is an illusion – in the negative sense of the term. In one sense, even if architecture wants to respond to a political program or fulfil social needs, it will never succeed because it is confronted, fortunately, by something that is also a black hole. And this black hole simply means that the 'masses' are still there and they are not at all recipients, or conscious, or reflected, or anything; it's an extremely perverse operator with respect to everything that is constructed. So even if architecture wants what it wants and tricks to signify what it wants to express, it will be deflected . . .

Fortunately, this is also the reason why we can continue to live in a universe that is as full, as determined, as functional as this. Our world would be unlivable without this power of innate deflection . . . However, I'm not sure that in the virtualized world of new technologies, information, and the media, this dualistic, indecipherable relationship of seduction will take place as it did before. It's possible that the secret you spoke about would be completely annihilated by another type of universe. It's also possible that in this universe of the virtual, which we talk about today, architecture wouldn't exist at all, that this symbolic form, which plays with weight, the gravity of things and their absence, their total transparency, would be abolished. No, I'm no longer sure this could occur in the virtual universe. We are completely screened in; the problem of architecture is expressed differently. So maybe there's a kind of completely superficial architecture that is confused with this universe. This would be an architecture of banality, of virtuality. It can be original as well, but it wouldn't be part of the same concept.

Values of functionalism

JN: We need to recognize that we're surrounded by a great deal of accidental architecture. And an entire series of modern, or modernist, attitudes – in the historical sense – have been founded on this particular reality. There are countless numbers of sites whose aesthetic lacks any sense of intention. We find this same phenomenon outside of architecture; it's a value of functionalism . . . The same applies to industrial zones at the end of the twentieth century, which are, for all intents and purposes, radical architectural forms, without concessions, abrupt, in which we can definitely locate a certain charm.

But I want to get back to your ideas about architecture, since you definitively expressed an opinion about it. For example . . . you wrote . . . 'New York is the epicenter of the world'. . .

New York or Utopia

[. . .]

JB: When I refer to New York as the epicenter of the end of the world,
I'm referring to an apocalypse. At the same time, it's a way of looking at it as a
realized utopia. This is the paradox of reality. We can dream about apocalypse,
but it's a perspective, something unrealizable, whose power lies in the fact that it
isn't realized. New York provides the kind of stupefaction characterized by a world
that is already accomplished, an absolutely apocalyptic world, but one that is
replete in its verticality – and in this sense, ultimately, it engenders a form of
deception because it is embodied, because it's already there, and we can no longer
destroy it. It's indestructible. The form is played out, it's outlived its own useful-
ness, it's been realized even beyond its own limits. There's even a kind of liberation,
a destructuring of space that no longer serves as a limit to verticality or, as in
other places, horizontality. But does architecture still exist when space has become
infinitely indeterminate in every dimension . . .

There's nothing better than New York. Other things will happen, and we'll
make the transition to a different universe, one that's much more virtual; but within
its order, we'll never do better than that city, that architecture, which is, at the
same time, apocalyptic. Personally, I like this completely ambiguous figure of the
city, which is simultaneously catastrophic and sublime, because it has assumed an
almost hieratic force . . .

JN: You also said something rather astonishing about architecture:
'Architecture is a mixture of nostalgia and extreme anticipation.' Do you recall?
Those ideas are still vital for me, but it's been fifteen years . . . Are they still vital
for you?

Architecture: between nostalgia and anticipation

JB: We're looking for the lost object, whether we're referring to
meaning or language. We use language, but it's always, at the same time, a form
of nostalgia, a lost object. Language in use is basically a form of anticipation,
since we're already in something else . . . We have to be in these two orders of

reality: we have to confront what we've lost and anticipate what's ahead of us; that's our brand of fatality ... But it's hard to understand because the idea of modernity is for all that the idea of a continuous dimension where it's clear that the past and the future coexist ... We ourselves may no longer be in that world – if we ever were! – for it may be no more than a kind of apparition. This seems to be true for any kind of form. Form is always already lost, then always already seen as something beyond itself. It's the essence of radicality ... It involves being radical in loss, and radical in anticipation – any object can be grasped in this way. My comments need to be contrasted with the idea that something could be 'real' and that we could consider it as having a meaning, a context, a subject, an object. We know that things are no longer like that, and even the things we take to be the simplest always have an enigmatic side, which is what makes them radical.

JN: I don't want to torture you any longer, but I'd like to read three other quotes: 'Architecture consists in working against a background of spatial deconstruction.' And 'All things are curves.' That's a very important sentence for me. And finally 'Provocation would be much too serious a form of seduction.' You said that in reference to architecture, by the way.

(Always) seduction. Provocation. Secrets

JB: ... 'All things are curves.' That's the easiest to start with because there are no end points or the end points connect in a curved mirror. All things, in this sense, fulfil their own cycle.

Provocation, seduction ... Programmed seduction doesn't exist, so it doesn't mean much. Seduction should, nevertheless, contain some sense of that antagonism, that countercurrent; it should both have the sense and implement it ... Here too any concerted effort at implementation is obviously contradictory. Seduction can't be programmed, and disappearance, whether of constructed things or generalized ambivalence, can't be officialized. It has to remain secret. The order of secrecy, which is the order of seduction, obviously exists only through provocation; it's almost exactly the opposite. Provocation is an attempt to make something visible through contradiction, through scandal, defiance; to make something visible that should perhaps guard its secret. The problem is to achieve this law or this rule. The rule is really the secret, and the secret obviously becomes increasingly difficult in a world like our own, where everything is given to us totally promiscuously, so that there are no gaps, no voids, no nothingness; nothingness no longer exists, and nothingness is where secrecy happens, the place where things lose their meaning, their identity – not only would they assume all possible meanings here, but they would remain truly unintelligible in some sense.

I think that in every building, every street, there is something that creates an event, and whatever creates an event is unintelligible. This can also occur in situations or in individual behaviour; it's something you don't realize, something you can't program. You have more experience than I do with urban projects, which arrange spatial freedom, the space of freedom; all those programs are obviously absolutely contradictory. So, at bottom, the secret exists wherever people hide it. It's also possible in dualistic, ambivalent relations, for at that moment something becomes unintelligible once again, like some precious material.

JN: We can continue by talking about the aesthetics of disappearance . . . You write, 'If being a nihilist is being obsessed by the mode of disappearance rather than the mode of production, then I'm a nihilist.' You also write, 'I am for everything that is opposed to culture.' This brings us back in a way to certain contemporary issues . . . I can say the same thing about architecture: I'm for everything that is opposed to architecture. Twenty years ago I began a book that way: 'The future of architecture is not architectural.' The key is to agree on what architecture is . . . and where it's going. The key is to agree on what culture is and where it's going.

The aesthetics of modernity

JB: I [refer] to culture in the sense of aestheticization, and I am opposed to such aestheticization because it inevitably involves a loss: the loss of the object, of this secret that works of art and creative effort might reveal and which is something more than aesthetics. The secret can't be aesthetically unveiled. It's the kind of 'punctum' Barthes spoke of in reference to photography – it's secret, something inexplicable and nontransmissible, something that is in no way interactive.

It's something that's there and not there at the same time. Within culture this thing is completely dissipated, volatilized. Culture involves the total legibility of everything in it, and what's more, it comes into being at the very moment Duchamp transposed a very simple object, the urinal, into an art object. He transposed its banality to create an event within the aesthetic universe and deaestheticize it. He forced banality upon it – he broke into the home of aesthetics – and stopped it cold. Paradoxically he made possible the generalized aestheticization that typifies the modern era. [Later] . . . [w]ith abstraction we had the impression that a liberation had taken place, an orgy of modernity. That all broke apart in a kind of sudden implosion, a levelling of the aesthetic's sense of the sublime. And in the end, when this aesthetic of the secret disappeared, we had culture.

A heroic architectural act?

JN: We might ask ourselves why there is no equivalent to Duchamp in the world of architecture. There is no equivalent because there is no auto-architecture. There is no architect who could make an immediate, scandalous gesture that was accepted. Architects have tried to confront these limits – that was the starting point of postmodernity. We could say that in his own way, Venturi tried to do it. He took the simplest building that existed, a basic building from the suburbs of Philadelphia – even the location wasn't important, it was the least significant location possible – made of brick, with standard windows, and so on, and he said: 'This is the architecture we must make today.' And his gesture implied an entire theory, a theory that was opposed to the heroic architectural act, although in terms of derision it was a 'weak' application of the Dadaist revolution (on the Richter scale, it was one or two; Duchamp is seven). But all these attempts culminated in notable failures, since we as architects are unable to attain the same distance from the object. I have no idea what would enable us to identify Duchamp's fountain if it weren't in a museographic space. It demands certain reading conditions and a certain distance, which don't exist for architecture. At most we could say that this act of complete vulgarization might occur in spite of the client's intentions. The only problem is that if you do that and you repeat it, it becomes insignificant. No further reality, no further reading of the act is possible; you've become part of the total disappearance of the architectural act.

JB: Duchamp's act also becomes insignificant, wants to be insignificant, wants insignificance, and becomes insignificant in spite of itself through repetition, as well as through all of Duchamp's by-products. The event itself is unique, singular, and that's the end of it. It's ephemeral. Afterward there's a whole string of them, in art as well, since from that moment on, the path was cleared for the resurgence of earlier forms; postmodernism, if you like. The moment simply existed.

Art, architecture and postmodernity

JN: So can this debate about contemporary art – 'it's junk, worthless' – be applied to architecture? Can it be extrapolated?

JB: I'd like to ask you the same thing.

JN: I'd say that the search for limits and the pleasure of destruction are part of both art and architecture. You were talking about the idea of destruction as something that can be positive. This search for a limit, this search for nothingness, almost nothingness, takes place within the search for something positive; that is, we're looking for the essence of something. This search for an essence reaches limits that are near the limits of perception and the evacuation of the visible. We no longer experience pleasure through the eye but through the mind. A white square on a white background is a type of limit. James Turrell is a type of limit. Does that mean it's worthless? In the case of James Turrell, you enter a space, and it's monochromatic. Is it one step further than Klein? Is that why you're fascinated? You know there's nothing there, you feel there's nothing there, you can even pass your hand through it, and you're fascinated by the object in a way because it's the essence of something. Once he's given us the keys to this game, he does the same thing with a square of blue sky. He's currently working on the crater of a volcano, where, when you lie down at the bottom of the crater, you can see the perfect circle of the cosmos. All of these ideas are based on a certain search for the limit of nothingness. So when you leave the Venice Biennale, realizing that this search for nothingness has ended in worthlessness, that's a critical judgement I can share in 80 per cent of the cases. However, the history of art has always consisted of a majority of minor works.

JB: This search for nothingness is, on the contrary, the aestheticized fact of wanting this nothingness to have an existence, a value, and even, at some point, a surplus value, without considering the market, which soon takes control of it. It's the opposite in one sense . . . Duchamp's gesture was to reduce things to insignificance. In a way, he's not responsible for what happened afterward. So when other artists take possession of this 'nothingness' or, through this nothingness, take possession of banality, waste, the world, the real world, and they transfigure the banal reality of the world into an aesthetic object, it's their choice, and it's worthless in that sense, but it's also annoying, because I would rather associate an aura with worthlessness, with 'nothingness.' This nothingness is in fact something. It's what hasn't been aestheticized. It's what, one way or another, can't be reduced to any form of aestheticization. Rather, it's this highly focused strategy of nothingness and worthlessness that I am opposed to. The difference between Warhol and the others, who did the same thing – although it isn't the same thing – is based on the fact that he takes an image and reduces it to nothing. He uses the technical medium to reveal the insignificance, the lack of objectivity, the illusion of the image itself. And then other artists make use of the technique to re-create an aesthetic in other technological media, through science itself, through scientific images. They reproduce the aesthetic. They do exactly the opposite of what Warhol was able to do, they reaestheticize the technique, while Warhol, through technique, revealed technique itself as a radical illusion.

Here the term 'worthlessness' is ambivalent, ambiguous. It can refer to the best or the worst. Personally, I assign great importance to worthlessness in the sense of nothingness, in the sense that, if we achieve this art of disappearance, we've achieved art, whereas all the strategy used to manage most of the stuff we're shown – where there's usually nothing to see in any event – serves precisely to convert that worthlessness into spectacle, into aesthetic, into market value, into a form of complete unconsciousness, the collective syndrome of aestheticization known as culture. We can't say it's all the same, but the exceptions can only be moments. For me, Duchamp is one of them; Warhol is another. But there are other singularities, Francis Bacon, perhaps, maybe others. But it's not a question of names of artists . . . It can never be anything but a onetime event that affects us in this world saturated with values and aesthetics. From that moment on, there is no more history of art. We see that art – and this is one aspect of its worth-lessness – with its retrograde history, exhausts itself in its own history trying to resuscitate all those forms, the way politics does in other areas. It's a form of regression, an interminable phase of repetition during which we can always bring back any older work of art, or style, or technique as a fashion or aesthetic – a process of endless recycling.

JN: . . . This has been a century of gigantic exploration: exploration of the real, exploration of sensations, of everything around us, a search for sensa-tions . . . But all that exploration kept getting extended further, and everyone is looking for whatever they can grab. Does this mean that all this exploration is part of that 'worthlessness'?

JB: Well, there may be a history of art that's not progressive but which deepens the analytic side of art, and all abstraction is still a reduction of the visible world, of the object, into its microelements. It's a way of returning to a primal geometry. It's exactly the same thing as the search for analytic truth in the social sciences. It's the same kind of process. We've gone from the evidence of appear-ances to the fundamental fractal nature of things. This is the history of abstraction, and this search leads directly into another dimension, which is no longer that of appearance or a strategy of appearances, but of a need centred on in-depth analytic knowledge of the object and the world, which, in a sense, puts an end to sense relations. It's the extermination of the sensible, but it still constitutes a search, I agree.

Once we've arrived at this point, however, it's over . . . We have an arti-ficial reconstruction of evidence, of perception, but the crucial act, the determining factor, is abstraction. Afterward we're no longer really in a world of forms; we're in a microworld. Art even anticipated scientific discovery; it went deeper and deeper into the fractal world, into geometry. I don't mean that all sensibility, all perception, disappeared. It's always possible for anyone, any object, to have a singular relation but not an aesthetic one, to have a primitive relation, something to do with this punctum, anyone can experience that . . . So-called aesthetic mediation is over with. The artist is someone who exploits the domain of singularity so that he can appropriate it and use it interactively both through the market structure and through a number of other things as well. But the dualistic relation of any individual with any object, even the most worthless, is singular, it retains its power, and it can be rediscovered. I don't feel that this has been lost; that's not the problem with the sensible, the fatal. By this I mean that the fatal relation with things, with appearances, can be rediscovered, but if it is, today that discovery will be in conflict with aesthetics, with art. In the same sense, you can rediscover a dualistic relation in society, in other domains, in alterity. But this doesn't take place through politics, or economics; those things are behind us, they have their history, and we are in another world where those mediating structures have either monopolized the entire market, and at that point should be destroyed, or have already destroyed themselves. By the way, that's what I meant when I said that 'art is worthless.'

Visual disappointment. Intellectual disappointment

[. . .]

JN: I have the impression that the sense of something's being 'worthless, worthless, worthless' in architecture also exists! It is just as overwhelming but, paradoxically, perhaps for the opposite reason. That is to say, what characterizes this worthless architecture today, three-quarters of the time, is the 'picturesque.' Or it's the extension of a private model of meaning and sensibility. One of the current dramas in architecture is modelling, cloning . . . [T]he majority of architectures produced today aren't based on those simple, clean, savage, radical rules that you talk about in your book on New York. Most of the time, they're a collage of objects, the one that presents the fewest problems either for the one who's designing it, or for the one who's receiving it, or for the builder. And for those three reasons, it's worthless, worthless, worthless. We're looking for something else.

Maybe we're looking for that aesthetic of disappearance that Paul Virilio discusses. But not necessarily in the sense Virilio intends, in that virtual, informatic space where information circulates rather than humans, not in a virtual space because those objects are completely lacking in meaning. That's the primary characteristic of everything being built today, and the paradox is that the most poetic things are, on the social level, the most dramatic. That is, the most authentic things, the truest, will be found in the cities of the South, where they are made out of necessity, but also in connection with a culture that's very much alive. These aren't objects that are parachuted in, inauthentic objects that correspond to some architectural convention. The problem of the worthlessness of architecture presents itself with at least the same acuity as in the field of art, but certainly not on the same basis.

The aesthetics of disappearance

JB: Obviously we need to be clear about what we mean by the aesthetics of disappearance . . . It's true that there are a thousand ways to disappear, but we can at least compare the kind of disappearance that results in extermination – which is one of the ideas underlying Paul Virilio's work – and the way things disappear in a 'network,' which affects all of us and could be considered a kind of sublimation. The disappearance I'm talking about, which results in the concept of worthlessness or nothingness I mentioned earlier, means that one form disappears into another. It's a kind of metamorphosis: appearance disappearance. The mechanism is completely different. It's not the same as disappearing within a network, where everyone becomes the clone or metastasis of something else; it's a chain of interlinked forms, into which we disappear, where everything implies its own disappearance. It's all about the art of disappearance. Unfortunately there's only one word to describe it, and the same is true for the term 'worthlessness.' We can use it in different senses, just as we can the term 'nothingness,' but no matter what happens, we enter a field of discourse that can no longer be fully explained, we've got to play the game, we're forced to.

Note

1.   Abridged version of 'First Interview' from *The Singular Objects of Archi-tecture* by Jean Baudrillard and Jean Nouvel; translated by Robert Bononno (University of Minnesota Press, 2002) pp 1–33. Originally published in French as *Les objets singuliers: Architecture et philosophie*. Copyright 2002 by Editions Calmann-Lévy. English translation copyright 2002 by Robert Bononno. Reprinted by permission.

Chapter Two

COOL CITIES

America [1]

Salt Lake City

Pompous Mormon symmetry. Everywhere marble: flawless, funereal (the Capitol, the organ in the Visitor Center). Yet a Los-Angelic modernity, too – all the requisite gadgetry for a minimalist, extraterrestrial comfort. The Christ-topped dome (all the Christs here are copied from Thorwaldsen's and look like Björn Borg) straight out of *Close Encounters*: religion as special effects. In fact, the whole city has the transparency and supernatural, otherworldly cleanness of a thing from outer space. A symmetrical, luminous, overpowering abstraction. At every intersection in the Tabernacle area – all marble and roses, and evangelical marketing – an electronic cuckoo-clock sings out: such Puritan obsessiveness is astonishing in this heat, in the heart of the desert, alongside this leaden lake, its waters also hyperreal from sheer density of salt. And, beyond the lake, the Great Salt Lake Desert where they had to invent the speed of prototype cars to cope with the absolute horizontality . . . But the city itself is like a jewel, with its purity of air and its plunging urban vistas more breathtaking even than those of Los Angeles. What stunning brilliance, what modern veracity these Mormons show, these rich bankers, musicians, international genealogists, polygamists (the Empire State in New York has something of this same funereal Puritanism raised to the

nth power). It is the capitalist, transsexual pride of a people of mutants that gives the city its magic, equal and opposite to that of Las Vegas, that great whore on the other side of the desert.

New York

More sirens here, day and night. The cars are faster, the advertisements more aggressive. This is wall-to-wall prostitution. And total electric light too. And the game – all games – gets more intense. It's always like this when you're getting near the centre of the world. But the people smile. Actually they smile more and more, though never to other people, always to themselves. [. . .]

The number of people here who think alone, sing alone, and eat and talk alone in the streets is mind-boggling. And yet they don't add up. Quite the reverse. They subtract from each other and their resemblance to one another is uncertain. [. . .]

Why do people live in New York? There is no relationship between them. Except for an inner electricity which results from the simple fact of their being crowded together. A magical sensation of contiguity and attraction for an artificial centrality. This is what makes it a self-attracting universe, which there is no reason to leave. There is no human reason to be here, except for the sheer ecstasy of being crowded together. [. . .]

By contrast with the American 'downtown areas' and their blocks of skyscrapers, La Défense has forfeited the architectural benefits of verticality and excess by squeezing its high-rise blocks into an Italian-style setting, into a closed theatre bounded by a ring-road. It is very much a garden *à la française*: a bunch of buildings with a ribbon around it. All this has closed off the possibility that these monsters might engender others to infinity, that they might battle it out within a space rendered dramatic by their very competition (New York, Chicago, Houston, Seattle, Toronto). It is in such a space that the pure architectural object is born, an object beyond the control of architects, which roundly repudiates the city and its uses, repudiates the interests of the collectivity and individuals and persists in its own madness. That object has no equivalent, except perhaps the arrogance of the cities of the Renaissance.

No, architecture should not be humanized. Anti-architecture, the true sort (not the kind you find in Arcosanti, Arizona, which gathers together all the 'soft' technologies in the heart of the desert), the wild, inhuman type that is beyond the measure of man was made here – made itself here – in New York, without considerations of setting, well-being, or ideal ecology. It opted for hard technologies, exaggerated all dimensions, gambled on heaven and hell . . . Eco-architecture, eco-society . . . this is the gentle hell of the Roman Empire in its decline.

Santa Barbara

On the aromatic hillsides of Santa Barbara, the villas are all like funeral homes. Between the gardenias and the eucalyptus trees, among the profusion of plant genuses and the monotony of the human species, lies the tragedy of a utopian dream made reality. In the very heartland of wealth and liberation, you always hear the same question: 'What are you doing after the orgy?' What do you do when everything is available – sex, flowers, the stereotypes of life and death? This is America's problem and, through America, it has become the whole world's problem.

All dwellings have something of the grave about them, but here the fake serenity is complete. The unspeakable house plants, lurking everywhere like the obsessive fear of death, the picture windows looking like Snow White's glass coffin, the clumps of pale, dwarf flowers stretched out in patches like sclerosis, the proliferation of technical gadgetry inside the house, beneath it, around it, like drips in an intensive care ward, the TV, stereo, and video which provide communication with the beyond, the car (or cars) that connect one up to that great shoppers' funeral parlour, the supermarket, and, lastly, the wife and children, as glowing symptoms of success . . . everything here testifies to death having found its ideal home.

Venice and Porterville

The obsessive fear of the Americans is that the lights might go out. Lights are left on all night in the houses. In the tower blocks the empty offices remain lit. On the freeways, in broad daylight, the cars keep all their headlights on. In Palms Ave., Venice, California, a little grocery store that sells beer in a part of town where no one is on the streets after 7 p.m. leaves its orange and green neon sign flashing all night, into the void. And this is not to mention the television, with its twenty-four-hour schedules, often to be seen functioning like a hallucination in the empty rooms of houses or vacant hotel rooms – as in the Porterville hotel where the curtains were torn, the water cut off, and the doors swinging in the wind, but on the fluorescent screen in each of the rooms a TV commentator was describing the take-off of the space shuttle. There is nothing more mysterious than a TV set left on in an empty room. It is even stranger than a man talking to himself or a woman standing dreaming at her stove. It is as if another planet is communicating with you. Suddenly the TV reveals itself for what it really is: a video of another world, ultimately addressed to no one at all, delivering its images indifferently, indifferent to its own messages (you can easily imagine it still functioning after humanity has disappeared). In short, in America the arrival of night-time or periods of rest cannot be accepted, nor can the Americans bear to see the technological process halted. Everything has to be working all the time, there has to be no let-up in man's artificial power, and the intermittent character of natural cycles (the seasons, day and night, heat and cold) has to be replaced by a functional continuum that is sometimes absurd (deep down, there is the same refusal of the intermittent nature of true and false: everything is true; and of good and evil: everything is good). You may seek to explain this in terms of fear, perhaps obsessional fear, or say that this unproductive expenditure is an act of mourning. But what is absurd is also admirable. The skylines lit up at dead of night, the air-conditioning systems cooling empty hotels in the desert and artificial light in the middle of the day all have something both demented and admirable about them. The mindless luxury of a rich civilization, and yet of a civilization perhaps as scared to see the lights go out as was the hunter in his primitive night. There is some truth in all of this. But what is striking is the fascination with artifice, with energy and space. And not only natural space: space is spacious in their heads as well.

Disneyland

[. . .] the cinema here is not where you think it is. It is certainly not to be found in the studios the tourist crowds flock to – Universal, Paramount, etc., those subdivisions of Disneyland. If you believe that the whole of the Western world is hypostatized in America, the whole of America in California, and California in MGM and Disneyland, then this is the microcosm of the West.

In fact what you are presented with in the studios is the degeneration of the cinematographic illusion, its mockery, just as what is offered in Disneyland is a parody of the world of the imagination. The sumptuous age of stars and images is reduced to a few artificial tornado effects, pathetic fake buildings, and childish tricks which the crowd pretends to be taken in by to avoid feeling too disappointed. Ghost towns, ghost people. The whole place has the same air of obsolescence about it as Sunset or Hollywood Boulevard. You come out feeling as though you have been put through some infantile simulation test. Where is the cinema? It is all around you outside, all over the city, that marvellous, continuous performance of films and scenarios. Everywhere but here.

It is not the least of America's charms that even outside the movie theatres the whole country is cinematic. The desert you pass through is like the set of a Western, the city a screen of signs and formulas. It is the same feeling you get when you step out of an Italian or a Dutch gallery into a city that seems the very reflection of the paintings you have just seen, as if the city had come out of the paintings and not the other way about. The American city seems to have stepped right out of the movies. To grasp its secret, you should not, then, begin with the city and move inwards to the screen; you should begin with the screen and move outwards to the city. It is there that cinema does not assume an exceptional form, but simply invests the streets and the entire town with a mythical atmosphere. That is where it is truly gripping. This is why the cult of stars is not a secondary phenomenon, but the supreme form of cinema, its mythical transfiguration, the last great myth of our modernity. Precisely because the idol is merely a pure, contagious image, a violently realized ideal. They say that stars give you something to dream about, but there is a difference between dreaming and fascination by images. The screen idols are immanent in the unfolding of life as a series of images. They are a system of luxury prefabrication, brilliant syntheses of the stereotypes of life and love. *They embody one single passion only: the passion for images*, and the immanence of desire in the image. They are not something to dream about; they are the dream. And they have all the characteristics of dreams: they produce a marked condensation (crystallization) effect and an effect of contiguity (they are immediately contagious), and, above all, they have that power of instantaneous visual materialization (*Anschaulichkeit*) of desire, which is also a feature of dreams. They do not, therefore, feed the romantic or sexual imagination; they are immediate visibility, immediate transcription, material collage, precipitation of desire. Fetishes, fetish objects, that have nothing to do with the world of the imagination, but everything to do with *the material fiction of the image*.

The Bonaventure Hotel

The top of the Bonaventure Hotel. Its metal structure and its plate-glass windows rotate slowly around the cocktail bar. The movement of the skyscrapers outside is almost imperceptible. Then you realize that it is the platform of the bar that is moving, while the rest of the building remains still. In the end I get to see the whole city revolve around the top of the hotel. A dizzy feeling, which continues inside the hotel as a result of its labyrinthine convolution. Is this still architecture, this pure illusionism, this mere box of spatio-temporal tricks? Ludic and hallucinogenic, is this postmodern architecture?

No interior/exterior interface. The glass facades merely reflect the environment, sending back its own image. This makes them much more formidable than any wall of stone. It's just like people who wear dark glasses. Their eyes are hidden and others see only their own reflection. Everywhere the transparency of interfaces ends in internal refraction. Everything pretentiously termed 'communication' and 'interaction' – Walkman, dark glasses, automatic household appliances, high-tech cars, even the perpetual dialogue with the computer – ends up with each monad retreating into the shade of its own formula, into its self-regulating little corner and its artificial immunity. Blocks like the Bonaventure building claim to be perfect, self-sufficient miniature cities. But they cut themselves off from the city more than they interact with it. They stop seeing it. They refract it like a dark surface. And you cannot get out of the building itself. You cannot fathom out its internal space, but it has no mystery; it is just like those games where you have to join all the dots together without any line crossing another. Here too everything connects, without any two pairs of eyes ever meeting.

The realized utopia

America is the original version of modernity. We are the dubbed or sub-titled version. America ducks the question of origins; it cultivates no origin or mythical authenticity; it has no past and no founding truth. Having known no primitive accumulation of time, it lives in a perpetual present. Having seen no slow, centuries-long accumulation of a principle of truth, it lives in perpetual simulation, in a perpetual present of signs. It has no ancestral territory. The Indians' territory is today marked off in reservations, the equivalent of the galleries in which America stocks its Rembrandts and Renoirs. But this is of no importance – America has no identity problem. In the future, power will belong to those peoples with no origins and no authenticity who know how to exploit that situation to the full. Look at Japan, which to a certain extent has pulled off this trick better than the US itself, managing, in what seems to us an unintelligible paradox, to transform the power of territoriality and feudalism into that of deterritoriality and weightlessness. Japan is already a satellite of the planet Earth. But America was already in its day a satellite of the planet Europe. Whether we like it or not, the future has shifted towards artificial satellites. [. . .]

The society's 'look' is a self-publicizing one. The American flag itself bears witness to this by its omnipresence, in fields and built-up areas, at service stations, and on graves in the cemeteries, not as a heroic sign, but as the trade-mark of a good brand. It is simply the label of the finest successful international enterprise, the US. This explains why the hyperrealists were able to paint it naively, without either irony or protest (Jim Dine in the 1960s), in much the same way as Pop Art gleefully transposed the amazing banality of consumer goods on to its canvases. There is nothing here of the fierce parodying of the American anthem by Jimi Hendrix, merely the light irony and neutral humour of things that have become banal, the humour of the mobile home and the giant hamburger on the sixteen-foot long billboard, the pop and hyper humour so characteristic of the atmosphere of America, where things almost seem endowed with a certain indulgence towards their own banality. But they are indulgent towards their own craziness too. Looked at more generally, they do not lay claim to being extraordinary; they simply are extraordinary. [. . .]

America is turning all this into reality and it is going about it in an uncontrolled, empirical way. All we do is dream and, occasionally, try and act out our dreams. America, by contrast, draws the logical, pragmatic consequences from everything that can possibly be thought. In this sense, it is naive and primitive; it knows nothing of the irony of concepts, nor the irony of seduction. It does not ironize upon the future or destiny: it gets on with turning things into material realities. To our utopian radicalism it counterposes its empirical radicalism, to which it alone gives dramatically concrete form. We philosophize on the end of lots of things, but it is here that they actually come to an end. It is here, for example, that territory has ceased to exist (though there is indeed a vast amount of space), here that the real and the imaginary have come to an end (opening all spaces up to simulation). It is here, therefore, that we should look for the ideal type of the end of our culture. It is the American way of life, which we think naive or culturally worthless, which will provide us with a complete graphic representation of the end of our values – which has vainly been prophesied in our own countries – on the grand scale that the geographical and mental dimensions of utopia can give to it.

But is this really what an achieved utopia looks like? Is this a successful revolution? Yes indeed! What do you expect a 'successful' revolution to look like? It is paradise. Santa Barbara is a paradise; Disneyland is a paradise; the US is a paradise. Paradise is just paradise. Mournful, monotonous, and superficial though it may be, it is paradise. There is no other. If you are prepared to accept the consequences of your dreams – not just the political and sentimental ones, but the theoretical and cultural ones as well – then you must still regard America today with the same naive enthusiasm as the generations that discovered the New World. That same enthusiasm which Americans themselves show for their own success, their own barbarism, their own power. If not, you have no understanding of the situation, and you will not be able to understand your own history – or the end of your history – either, because Europe can no longer be understood by starting out from Europe itself. The US is more mysterious: *the mystery of American reality* exceeds our fictions and our interpretations. The mystery of a society which seeks to give itself neither meaning nor an identity, which indulges neither in transcendence nor in aesthetics and which, for precisely that reason, invents the only great modern verticality in its buildings, which are the most grandiose manifestations within the vertical order and yet do not obey the rules of transcendence, which are the most prodigious pieces of architecture and yet do not obey the laws of aesthetics, which are ultra-modern and ultra-functional, but also have about them something non-speculative, primitive, and savage – a culture (or unculture) like this remains a mystery to us.

We are at home with introversion and reflexion, and with different effects of meaning coexisting under the umbrella of a concept. But the object freed from its concept, free to deploy itself in extraverted form, in the equivalence of all its effects . . . To us this is a total enigma. Extraversion is a mystery to us in exactly the same way as the commodity was to Marx: the commodity, hieroglyph of the modern world, mysterious precisely because it is extraverted, a form realizing itself in its pure operation and in pure circulation (hello Karl!). [. . .]

They [the Americans] have opened up the deserts, threaded and criss-crossed them with their freeways, but by some mysterious interaction their towns and cities have taken on the structure and colour of the desert. They have not destroyed space; they have simply rendered it infinite by the destruction of its centre (hence these infinitely extendable cities). In so doing, they have opened up a true fictional space. In the 'savage mind', too, there is no natural universe, no transcendence of either man or nature, or of history. Culture is everything, or nothing, depending on how you look at it. You find this same absence of distinction between the two in modern simulation. There is no natural universe there either, and you cannot differentiate between a desert and a metropolis. [. . .]

There is no culture here, no cultural discourse. No ministries, no commission, no subsidies, no promotion. There is none of the sickly cultural pathos which the whole of France indulges in, that fetishism of the cultural heritage, nor of our sentimental – and today also statist and protectionist – invocation of culture. The Beaubourg would be impossible here, just as it would in Italy (for other reasons). Not only does centralization not exist, but the idea of a cultivated culture does not exist either, no more than that of a theological, sacred religion. No culture of culture, no religion of religion. One should speak rather of an 'anthropological' culture, which consists in the invention of mores and a way of life. That is the only interesting culture here, just as it is New York's streets and not its museums or galleries that are interesting. Even in dance, cinema, the novel, fiction, and architecture, there is something wild in everything specifically American, something that has not known the glossy, high-flown rhetoric and theatricality of our bourgeois cultures, that has not been kitted out in the gaudy finery of cultural distinction.

Here in the US, culture is not that delicious panacea which we Europeans consume in a sacramental mental space and which has its own special columns in the newspapers – and in people's minds. Culture is space, speed, cinema, technology. This culture is authentic, if anything can be said to be authentic. This is not cinema or speed or technology as optional extra (everywhere in Europe you get a sense of modernity as something tacked on, heterogeneous, anachronistic). In America cinema is true because it is the whole of space, the whole way of life that are cinematic. The break between the two, the abstraction which we deplore, does not exist: life is cinema. [. . .]

When the Americans transfer Roman cloisters to the New York Cloysters, we find this unforgivably absurd. Let us not make the same mistake by transferring our cultural values to America. We have no right to such confusion. In a sense, they do because they have space, and their space is the refraction of all others. When Paul Getty gathers Rembrandts, Impressionists, and Greek statues together in a Pompeian villa on the Pacific coast, he is following American logic, the pure baroque logic of Disneyland. He is being original; it is a magnificent stroke of cynicism, naivety, kitsch, and unintended humour – something astonishing in its nonsensicality. Now the disappearance of aesthetics and higher values in kitsch and hyperreality is fascinating, as is the disappearance of history and the real in the televisual. It is in this unfettered pragmatics of values that we should find some pleasure. If you simply remain fixated on the familiar canon of high culture, you miss the essential point (which is, precisely, the inessential). [. . .]

No desire: the desert. Desire is still something deeply natural, we live off its vestiges in Europe, and off the vestiges of a moribund critical culture. Here the cities are mobile deserts. No monuments and no history: the exaltation of mobile deserts and simulation. There is the same wildness in the endless, indifferent cities as in the intact silence of the Badlands. Why is LA, why are the deserts so fascinating? It is because you are delivered from all depth there – a brilliant, mobile, superficial neutrality, a challenge to meaning and profundity, a challenge to nature and culture, an outer hyperspace, with no origin, no reference-points.

No charm, no seduction in all this. Seduction is elsewhere, in Italy, in certain landscapes that have become paintings, as culturalized and refined in their design as the cities and museums that house them. Circumscribed, traced-out, highly seductive spaces where meaning, at these heights of luxury, has finally become adornment. It is exactly the reverse here: there is no seduction, but there is an absolute fascination – the fascination of the very disappearance of all aesthetic and critical forms of life in the irradiation of an objectless neutrality. Immanent and solar. The fascination of the desert: immobility without desire. Of Los Angeles: insane circulation without desire. The end of aesthetics.

It is not just the aesthetics of decor (of nature or architecture) that vanishes into thin air, but the aesthetics of bodies and language [. . .]

What is arresting here is the absence of all these things – both the absence of architecture in the cities, which are nothing but long tracking shots of signals, and the dizzying absence of emotion and character in the faces and bodies. Handsome, fluid, supple, or cool, or grotesquely obese, probably less as a result of compulsive bulimia than a general incoherence, which results in a casualness about the body or language, food or the city: a loose network of individual, successive functions, a hypertrophied cell tissue proliferating in all directions.

Thus the only tissue of the city is that of the freeways, a vehicular, or rather an incessant transurbanistic, tissue, the extraordinary spectacle of these thousands of cars moving at the same speed, in both directions, headlights full on in broad daylight, on the Ventura Freeway, coming from nowhere, going nowhere: an immense collective act, rolling along, ceaselessly unrolling, without aggression, without objectives – transferential sociality, doubtless the only kind in a hyperreal, technological, soft-mobile era, exhausting itself in surfaces, networks, and soft technologies. No elevator or subway in Los Angeles. No verticality or underground, no intimacy or collectivity, no streets or facades, no centre or monuments: a fantastic space, a spectral and discontinuous succession of all the various functions, of all signs with no hierarchical ordering – an extravaganza of indifference, extravaganza of undifferentiated surfaces – the power of pure open space, the kind you find in the deserts. The power of the desert form: it is the erasure of traces in the desert, of the signified of signs in the cities, of any psychology in bodies. An animal and metaphysical fascination – the direct fascination of space, the immanent fascination of dryness and sterility. [. . .]

Its definition is absolute, its frontier initiatory, its ridges steep, its contours cruel. It is a place of signs of an imperious necessity, an ineluctable necessity – but void of all meaning, arbitrary and inhuman, and one crosses it without deciphering them. Irrevocable transparency. The towns of the desert also end abruptly; they have no surround. And they have about them something of the mirage, which may vanish at any instant. You have only to see Las Vegas, sublime Las Vegas, rise in its entirety from the desert at nightfall bathed in phosphorescent lights, and return to the desert when the sun rises, after exhausting its intense, superficial energy all night long, still more intense in the first light of dawn, to understand the secret of the desert and the signs to be found there: a spellbinding discontinuity, an all-enveloping, intermittent radiation.

The secret affinity between gambling and the desert: the intensity of gambling reinforced by the presence of the desert all around the town. The air-conditioned freshness of the gaming rooms, as against the radiant heat outside. The challenge of all the artificial lights to the violence of the sun's rays. Night of gambling sunlit on all sides; the glittering darkness of these rooms in the middle of the desert. Gambling itself is a desert form, inhuman, uncultured, initiatory, a challenge to the natural economy of value, a crazed activity on the fringes of exchange. But it too has a strict limit and stops abruptly; its boundaries are exact, its passion knows no confusion. Neither the desert nor gambling are open areas; their spaces are finite and concentric, increasing in intensity toward the interior, toward a central point, be it the spirit of gambling or the heart of the desert – a privileged, immemorial space, where things lose their shadow, where money loses its value, and where the extreme rarity of traces of what signals to us there leads men to seek the instantaneity of wealth.

C o o l   M e m o r i e s   I   (1 9 8 0 – 8 5)[2]

Urbino. Gubbio. Mantua

The beauty of these low doors opening on to successive rooms, the slipping of these perfect rectangles one inside the other. A violent eroticism produced by the geometric and hierarchical regularity of the buildings. Moving from one room to another, changing spaces is erotic. Not sexual: but belonging to that ideality of seduction in which the difference between the sexes appears like a subtle and aesthetic clue to the duality of things, an innovation, a surprise, before the Manichean violence of sex irrupts.

Trieste[3]

Here European nihilism takes on the charm of those autumn vines that plunge into the sea, under the southerly wind, from karstic cliffs. On the cliffs' horizon, oil refineries blaze like the final solution. Some concepts that are too fluid to linger long on the scene turn on the crest of the waves, on the ironic transparency of the sea.

Palermo

The way they drive there conforms to the cruel ceremonial of provocative, animal dancing. It is a challenge verging upon the lethal limit of suicide, but one in which eliding the act preserves the rules of the game. Animals confront each other in this way, to establish supremacy without actually inflicting harm. The violent rhetoric of *hard driving*,[4] and indeed all the town's scenography are products of this continual dicing with death.

Watching for six centuries over this archaic ceremonial, which sends modernity nowhere. The day should simply break, and then immediately come to an end. Things should just appear, and be immediately abolished.

Pompeii

Pompeii: we are indebted to a catastrophe for having preserved the most extraordinary piece of our classical heritage. But for Vesuvius we would not have had this living hallucination of Antiquity. As we owe the preservation of mammoths to the sudden onset of the Ice Age. Today, it is all our artificial memory systems that play the museum-building role of natural disasters.

Montreal

In just one week, winter, spring and summer following one after the other. Hence the dreamy mists of the St Lawrence, caused by the tepid rain falling on the ice. On the other side of the lake, the Indian village takes on the dramatic form of the Great North, of exile and snow. But here, in the city, everything takes on the dramatic form of ennui. There are two forms of energy in Montreal, the electric energy of the Great Lakes and the psychological energy of monotony.

Tower blocks

There is something archaic in tall buildings and tower blocks heroically defying gravity. It is easier to imagine tower blocks only starting at the fifteenth floor because that is the point where they become interesting. Or even a style of architecture which would begin on the surface of the sky and reach down towards the ground in unequal lunges, and no doubt would not end there. Theory should do the same and start out from the end of things, from their presumed altitude and move back down towards their 'reality', but not even stop there, for that is only an imaginary line.

If we want theory to run on to infinity on both sides of reality, we should knock down the first fifteen storeys right away . . .

Vélizy

All those shepherds in the Pyrenees who are being fitted out with fibre optics, radio relay stations and cable TV. Obviously the stakes are pretty high! And not just in social terms. Did these people think they were already living in society, with their neighbours, their animals, their stories? What a scandalously underdeveloped condition they were in, what a monstrous deprivation of all the blessings of information, what barbaric solitude they were kept in, with no possibility of expressing themselves, or anything.

Vélizy 2

We used to leave them in peace. If they were called on, it was to get them to come and die in the towns, in the factories or in a war. Why have we suddenly developed a need for them, when they have no need of anything? What do we want them to serve as witnesses of? Because we'll force them to if we have to: the new terror has arrived, not the terror of 1984, but that of the twenty-first century. The new negritude has arrived, the new servitude. There is already a roll-call of the martyrs of information. The Bretons whose TV pictures are restored as soon as possible after the relay stations have been blown up . . . Vélizy . . . in the Pyrenees. The new guinea pigs. The new hostages. Crucified on the altar of information, pilloried at their consoles. Buried alive under information. All this to make them admit the inexpressible service that is being done to them, to extort from them a confession of their sociality, of their 'normal' condition as associated anthropoids.

Versailles. St Peter

The Dream: a heavy lorry carrying a block of hewn marble collides with the columns of a building which looks like Versailles or St Peter's, Rome. The lorry overturns and the driver gets out, cursing. In the meantime, the whole facade of the building sways and slowly collapses. And, at that point, like rats leaving a sinking ship, all the statues, which up till then had remained motionless in their various positions, upright, stooping, or leaning back, slowly begin to wake, to stir, to open their eyes and run off to escape the disaster. Were they human beings who had been playing this role for centuries? They had been waiting for the end to break free.

The Pompidou Centre

Beaubourg: the sacred rubbish-heap of stockpiled values (the fifth floor) – the desacralized rubbish-heap of free expression (the piazza). Added to which today is a heap of real rubbish caused by a strike among the maintenance staff. A logical strike this, since its demand is that the management of refuse disposal be included in culture (there is at this very moment an exhibition of refuse at Beaubourg) and that the staff should be directly employed by the institution. Yet the latter, for all its devotion to mobility, versatility and the absorption of the heteroclite, seems incapable of mastering this situation. It will die, therefore, of its own waste, and in so doing serve as a model to postmodern civilization. Beaubourg is destined to exercise the fascination of dead centres, to suffer pestilence and pillage. It is an object that is wrecked before it even begins, a monument to continual absorption and evacuation, an involutive, voracious, fractal zone, where parasitisms are pushed to the limit and lines of demarcation vanish, giving way simply to the incestuous virulence of the multitude fallen prey to itself. Let us leave it this spectral quality of putrid object, condemned to rapid degradation – the only modern object we have produced, unintentionally.

Urban monsters

What sense would there be in blending in these urban monsters (Beaubourg, La Villette, La Défense, Opéra, Bastille, etc.) with the city or the surrounding area? They are not monuments; they are monsters. They testify not to the integrity of the city but to its disintegration, not to its organic nature but to its disorganization. They do not provide a rhythm for the city and its exchanges; they are projected on to it like extraterrestrial objects, like spacecraft falling to earth from some dark catastrophe. Neither centre nor periphery, they mark out a false centrality and around them lies a false sphere of influence; in reality they reflect the satellization of urban existence. Their attraction serves only to impress the tourists, and their function, like that of airports and places of interchange in general, is that of a place of expulsion, extradition, and urban ecstasy. Moreover, this is what all the alternative groups and the subculture that congregate there are primarily looking for: an empty ecstasy, an iccfloe in outer space, a cosmopolitan strand, a parasitic site . . . we must take them as they are – monsters they are; monsters we must leave them.

Paris

In the early morning and the semiconsciousness of awakening, in this quiet street, which affluence lends a provincial charm even though it is in the very heart of Paris, there is suddenly a solitary sound, which appears to rise up from the depths of your dreams: the shrill clatter of the high heels of a woman whom the daily coming of the light sends scurrying toward her work. The sound begins at the end of the street, grows as she passes beneath the window, in a great hurry, merciless in the morning light (nobody would ever walk like this at night) then dies away towards the other end. She took an eternity to walk the length of this street, though it is not long, so harshly did the indomitable metallic reverberation seem to condemn the noiseless, sleepy world all around. I am sure that the woman was well aware of this, and that it was the only pleasure of her day.

Berlin

All of a sudden, I'm right there in front of it without having realized. A long line of graffiti runs right across it, like the graffiti in the New York subway, like the West's mania for stickers. Suddenly, I have no historical imagination to cope with this wall, with this city cut in two like a brain severed by an artificial scalpel. The buildings which border upon it bear the charred traces of a hot history – cold history, for its part, feeds on cold signs, which reduce the imagination to despair (even graffiti are cold signs; the only funny signs are the rabbits hopping about in the barbed-wire friezes of *no-man's-land*).[5]

Impossible to feel the old thrill of terror. Everything is meaningless. Here at the summit of history, dismantled by its very violence, all is calm and spectral like a piece of waste ground in November. Any old abandoned inner-city area would offer the same spectacle. What is striking is the museification of history as waste ground. The men who fought the battles remember them, like a nightmare or, in other words, like something which is at least the realization of a desire, but now signs are the real battlefield. It is they that are the conductors of lethal energy, they that electrocute. Today, it is circuits which burn – the circuits in the brain, the circuits in the sensory, loving machines that we are. It is no longer buildings which burn or cities which are laid waste; it is the radio relays of our memories you can hear crackling.

I gaze in stupefaction at this wall and cannot summon anything from my memory. I am as helpless to find anything as those who will look at it in two thousand years' time no doubt will be to make any historical sense of it. Mentally closing my eyes, I see Christo's wall, the huge veil of fabric strung across the hills of California . . . Where does this passion to unfurl bands and walls come from – here this strip of concrete, elsewhere magnetic tapes or the unravellings scientists dream of – of strings of chromosomes or the spirals of DNA? In their very hearts, their inner convolutions, things are wound around upon themselves: we should not try to sort out the imbroglio. Here the labyrinth of a city, and, at the same time, the Gordian knot of history, have been destroyed at a stroke by a lethal incision. None of this heals over – but the pain itself is forgotten.

Rome in December

The gentle air of the Piazza Navona in December, with the acetylene lamps and the reflections of the turquoise water on the Bernini horses. A beauty that is purely Roman. In the Campo dei Fiori someone has laid fresh flowers at the foot of the statue of Giordano Bruno, burned for heresy on this very spot four centuries ago. The touching loyalty of the Roman people; where else would you see such a thing? The hot December multitudes spill out into the street: Christmas is almost as mild here as in Brazil. The city is only beautiful when the crowd invades it. So many people on the streets always gives the impression of a silent uprising. Everyone walks alone in the luminous muted buzz of voices and the narrow streets. Everything is transformed into a silent opera, a theatrical geometry. Everything sings in this part of the city.

Night on the cities

Rome, Berlin, Sydney, New York, Rio. My secretarial staff is expanding. My rainbow too. The night which would fall simultaneously on all the cities of the world has not yet occurred. The sun which would illuminate all the cities of the world at once has not yet risen.

Every woman is like a time zone. She is a nocturnal fragment of your journey.

She brings you unflaggingly closer to the next night.

Some women have disguised themselves as Congolese dugouts or Aleutian pearls.

Why shouldn't they disguise themselves as a time zone, or even as the ecstasy of the journey? Everywhere there is pleasure you will find woman in disguise, her features lost or metamorphosed into the ecstasy of things. Everywhere there is a woman dying.

Dunkirk

The excited crowds, the champagne corks popping, the old workers weeping at the launch of the last ship from the dockyard. A mass celebration of the end of work. For nobody actually wants this enormous ship. It is a pure act. It does not even have a name. They did not even dare to baptize it since it is the fruit of the conjoint sterility of Land and Labour, as Marx would say – and I wouldn't mind seeing his face if he could view this bewildering product of the productive forces. It has been given the code number 331. It will merely have served as a pretext for the mania for production, the futile passion for production which still survives today to drive generations to despair. This fabulous object, a testament to the immense useless capacity of man, should immediately be put away in a museum, in a crypt of neon, together with all the workers who are now slaves not of capital, but merely of the legend of work, and who have, in their own lifetimes, become part of the legend of the factories.

Ideal City

The Ideal Woman is like the Città Ideale. A pure, deserted form, with a few blinds raised to reveal a cool and meaningless shade, with a few houseplants poking out, and sometimes an allegorical item of linen.

Fifth Avenue

Little tribal ceremony among intellectuals on Fifth Avenue to discuss the end of the world. It might seem a terrific idea to talk about this in New York of all places since this is the world's epicentre, but, on reflection, there is no sense in the idea, since New York already is the end of the world. There is no sense reflecting on this in miniature in a scenario which is necessarily inferior to its model. Except the very requirement that we should rescue the *idea* of the end of the world from its real occurrence – which is the habitual labour of intellectuals.

Suburban comfort

Towns are never left alone; there are always works going on – digging, demolition, construction. Knocking down, building up again. Perhaps only certain places in California, completely anaesthetized by domestic luxury and suburban comfort, seem to have come to rest in a fixed and lasting ambience, beyond this perpetual deconstruction. Works are always going on in our bodies too. They are constantly being disturbed, tortured, renovated. Never at rest, never serene. Peace of mind – impossible to keep it more than a few hours. Impatience always gets the upper hand. Everyone aspires to peace and quiet, but they do so today in a thoroughly derisory manner, wherein we see the last moments of the contemplative soul. In the countryside there is always a dog howling. And sterility is hereditary.

Cool Memories II (1987–90) [6]

American towns

Old towns and cities have a history; American ones, being veritable urban bombs with no consideration for planning, have an uncontrolled sprawl. New towns have neither. They dream of an impossible past and of an explosion which is itself improbable.

Rio [7]

Morning sun shines on the planes, on the hills of Rio. The airport is full of zombies, of orphan souls. But a faint glow still lends charm to this stopover.

Buenos Aires [8]

Here, in Buenos Aires, it's the last tango of French thought. Moribund at home, but lascivious and ferocious in other latitudes, it still dances its nostalgic tango. Everywhere it makes its agony at being exported productive, and regenerates itself with fresh and cosmopolitan energies. It is a new empire of colonial signs.

Puerto Stroessner

Tourist hell. Asphalt in the jungle, the great stampede for fakes. Everything is fake, from the cameras to the perfumes and the drugs – right down to the advertisements warning visitors to beware of imitations. But this in no way detracts from the sublimeness of the cataracts.

Sites of fascination

If I've understood the distinction you've been making for ten (twenty?) years between seduction (the Italian landscape, the theatre, meaning, etc.) and fascination (American highways, the desert, absence of culture, the void, the media), I believe that, by also describing the sites of fascination, where meaning is supposed to implode with a great flourish, you bestow beauty on that void and give meaning to what shouldn't have any. And yet there is no contradiction in all this, since it's clear that the literary endeavour by which, in spite of oneself, one lends meaning to works of art (in which one does one's utmost to show they elude all interpretation) is, quite simply, art criticism.

So it could be said you're an art critic who isn't interested in art, but takes the real (the hyperreal, the freeways, television, etc.) for a work of art, with all that that implies in terms of sensitive, spectatorly, carnal, visual to the most 'lived' details by which you flesh out what are ultimately your metaphysical musings. Hence, your success with those in the plastic arts who, in their turn, are so feeble-minded as to take your metaphors literally and haven't understood that, in taking simulation as a mode, they are no longer engaged in simulation.

Venice (California)

The slender palm trees of Security Pacific against a white background, the painted walls, Venice (California), the mirror-glass buildings all bear witness to the intelligence of this city, which has not ceased to reflect itself in spite of its stunning growth (which is not true of the megalopolises of South America).

Los Angeles

Here in LA at seven in the morning, the whole city is active. The light is total and the people totally active. There is something as magic in this early morning excitement as there is in the agitation of the night. Even when suburbanized, people here have maintained a pioneering – or animal – rhythm: they eat early, go to bed early, rise early. It's true that the morning hours are the finest. After that comes the smog, the vitreous humour of the afternoon. And then again towards evening. The gentle light, the violet shadows of the tower blocks.

Marilyn's grave[9]

A box in a wall. Faintly disappointing. Why not a real grave? A mauve tower block serves as its monument, dominating the Westwood cemetery. Before that it was a bank that towered over the graves. A bank called 'Perpetual Savings'.

Salt Lake City. Las Vegas

The translucency of Christ and religion is to Salt Lake what the spectral ritual of gambling and money is to Las Vegas. The biblical, evangelical, genealogical, operational compulsion of the Mormons is to faith what the calculating, superstitious madness of the Las Vegas addicts is to money. Messianism and discipleship reach perfection at Salt Lake City. Heresy and apostasy are at their height at Las Vegas.

Disneyworld

At Disneyworld in Florida they are building a giant mock-up of Hollywood, with the boulevards, studios, etc. One more spiral in the simulacrum. One day they will rebuild Disneyland at Disneyworld.

Beyond Las Vegas

To disappear there, in the depths of some motel, in some Nevada gambling town. How long would it take for someone to react, to get anxious, to find me . . . This would be fantastic. The temptation of not existing for anyone, of demonstrating you don't exist for anyone. This is the hostage complex – the hostage in whom everyone very rapidly loses interest. A puerile fantasy: to check that someone loves you. Something you should never try. No one comes through this ordeal.

Venice (California). New York. Lisbon

You have to be a perfect dancer to dance immobility, like these solitary breakdancers on the sidewalks of Venice (California), New York and Lisbon. Their bodies only move at long intervals, like the hand of a clock stopping for a minute on every second, spending an hour on each position. This is freeze-act, as elsewhere one finds freeze-phrase (the fragment which fixes the writing) or the freeze-frame in the cinema, which fixes the movement of the entire city. This immobility is not an inertia, but a paroxysm which boils movement down into its opposite. The same dialectic was already present in Chinese opera or in animal dances – an art of stupor, slowness, bewitchment. This is the art of the photograph too, where the unreal pose wins out over real movement and the 'dissolve', with the result that a more intense, more advanced stage of the image is achieved in photography today than in cinema.

Shop windows

The thousands of shop windows which are the intestinal flora of the city.

Shop windows 2

In the shop window there gleams an agate ring left five years ago by an unknown female client. Opposite, in the antique shop, amid a jumble of rare objects, a Regency clock stands dreamily, indicating the phases of the moon and the slightest nuances of time in this timeless city. A city which keeps intact the secret promiscuity of rich and poor.

Arche de la Défense

There can be no finer proof that the distress of the rest of the world is at the root of Western power and that the spectacle of that distress is its crowning glory than the inauguration, on the roof of the Arche de la Défense, with a sumptuous buffet laid on by the Fondation des Droits de l'Homme, of an exhibition of the finest photos of world poverty. Should we be surprised that spaces are set aside in the Arche d'Alliance[10] for universal suffering hallowed by caviar and champagne?

Coupole

And why don't I go to the demo any more? And why don't I go to the Coupole? For the same reason. Both are too well stewarded. There's no sky above the Coupole any more, there's no cupola above the Coupole, there's no sky above the demo, there's no demo in the demo, the stewarding is too tight instead of going to the Coupole, you watch it from the other side of the boulevard. Instead of going to the demo, you watch it from the terrace of the Coupole.

São Paulo

São Paulo – nonchalance and frenzy.

Like the sky: luminous and smoky – the traffic: dreamily violent.

A strident pathway down the sweep of the avenues.

A strident pathway through the hazy mix of races.

Copacabana

The rich ruling class of Copacabana keeps itself shut away by its slaves. Those slaves who peacefully, silently devour the space-time of the masters, who forbid access, even in dreams, to those luxurious apartments, who hold the keys to their souls as they hold the keys to their personal elevators.

Cool Memories III (1992–95)[11]

Venice

If Venice with its ramifications, its little alleyways, its interlaced spaces, could open out all its twists and turns like the convolutions of a cerebral hemisphere, it would occupy an infinite space. The equivalent, perhaps, of New York. And perhaps New York, by miniaturizing its circuits, could rediscover the labyrinthine charm of Venice. The one is the site of an indifferent antagonism, the other the privilege of a deferred death-agony.

Puerto Vallarta

The great condominiums being built under arc lights in the tropical forest of Puerto Vallarta: *de luxe* penitentiaries, elements for a final solution, like the refineries at Galveston or the Santa Barbara oil rigs.

Bern. Zurich

The cities of Switzerland are the most squeaky-clean, the healthiest, the best-protected on earth, and even the old parts have such a brand-new air about them you would think they had been reconstructed, whereas they have in fact never been destroyed. Yet it is in these cities – Bern, Zurich – that the hardest '*öffentliche Drogenszene*' is to be found. Drugs are present everywhere, like the intravenous heroin of that wealth. The gold of the depths feeds the canker on the surface.

Brasilia

In the recording studio, your thoughts parade as though on a teleprompter. You become the 'auto-reader' of your own ideas. Especially if you happen to glance at the monitor, where you see yourself talking in real time.

In a television studio, you feel your ideas emptying of their wit, of that kind of quality which one finds (if at all) only in a relation of seduction or rivalry. One is witty only in alterity, even if one has ideas in solitude.

Wit in this sense – the disturbing, surprising, charming effects of ideas – functions only within a dual, sensual game between minds. Something which the virtuality of the screen and of the millions of spectators prevents. The screen is a form of frozen, confiscated alterity – ideal alterity, perhaps, like the alterity of the Ideal City, in which there is no one.

Brasilia's satellites

In the satellite towns around Brasilia, which lies on a plateau that is supposed to be the world's magnetic centre of gravity, and in magical Arizona, its quartz substratum generating extraterrestrial vibrations, the human being everywhere invents cult places, cult objects, akin to cargo cults or Aztec sanctuaries, which are allotted the role of attracting the attention of a higher species of whatever kind. We are obsessed with the idea of being discovered, and live in fear of not being, or of having disappeared before it can happen. Biosphere 2 is a kind of mind-boggling preparation for that encounter of the third kind. Like messages launched into space or space modules loaded up with the emblems of humanity (Bach's music, etc.).

The Aztecs also lived in hope of encountering a higher race. But the Spaniards, when they arrived, exterminated them. Fortunately for us, no other race can be seen emerging on our horizon (though perhaps there is one emerging from within the depths of our own).

Free zones' farce

The obscenity of the free zones, the tax-exempt zones, those frontier zones surrendered to the total vulgarity of commodities, is also to be found in the pedestrian precincts of modern cities. The extradition of the car ought to gladden our hearts. And yet we feel it to be an even worse farce, given the effort to fool us with the pretence of a city with a human face, whereas what is sublime about cities is quite clearly their inhuman character and, in particular, the vital alienation of car traffic.

American campuses

Like Disneyland, they are an ideal micro-city, the artificial ideal type of an intellectual biosphere. Like any realization of an ideal, they end up secreting a fierce coercion ('political correctness') and an internal intoxication, with its poisons and endorphins.

Pointe du Raz

One day at the Pointe du Raz, on the rocky plateau looking out on to the Baie des Trépassés,[12] the erratic tourists move around, far apart from each other, like contemporary stand-ins for shipwrecked souls.

Copacabana

Thousands of bodies everywhere. In fact, just one body: a single immense ramified mass of flesh, all sexes merged. A single, shameless, expanded human polyp, a single organism, in which all collude like the sperm in seminal fluid. The lack of distinction between the town and the beach brings the primal scene more or less directly into the public arena. The sexual act is permanent, but not in the sense of Nordic eroticism: it is in the epidermal promiscuity, the confusion of bodies, lips, buttocks, hips – a single fractal entity disseminated beneath the membrane of the sun.

This human hyperorganism puts one in mind of that other huge organic individual in Canada – the world's largest – made up of 45,000 aspens, all sharing, through their mingled roots, in the same telluric life, the whole forest constituting a single vegetal entity. In the same way, all these Brazilian bodies make up a kind of single being, living the same life, with the same fluids coursing through them, aquiver with the same passions. What social or political status can there be for an entity of this order?

Montreal. Rio

From the Montreal snowstorm to the Rio heatwave: the diagonal of the perfect journey. From underground complexes designed to last our six months of winter to thoroughfares seething with naked bodies and an insane level of traffic. From respectful, moral comfort to warm, wild confusion. From consensual, air-conditioned space to sensual, tropical space. From human difference, made up of multiculturalism and tolerance, to animal intolerance, composed of unself-consciousness and violence.

The only common factor between the northern and southern hemispheres is that generation you see everywhere, in all latitudes, running, jogging or walking, and high on phobic concern for their bodies. This is the New International Hygienic Order, the order of the repressed and the disembodied of modern society, of the disabled of the Virtual, who always seem to have just escaped from their wheelchairs and to be on the point of returning to them. This is the hygiene of the Assassins.

Pompeii

We learn that, at the moment of the catastrophe, Pompeii was peopled only by squatters and poor people, by old women and degenerates. Another fine dream gone! The thought that a natural catastrophe might just once have struck the rich first – or even rich and poor indiscriminately – is yet another we must relinquish. God never gets it wrong. Only the *Titanic* remains, but one day we shall learn that it was only carrying emigrants whose path to Eldorado was cut off by a providential iceberg.

Luxembourg Gardens

This statue in the Luxembourg Gardens which I find infinitely seductive. It is the statue of a naked girl, reclining against an obelisk and delicately holding in her left hand a strange object elegantly directed towards her nubile sex – the whole doubtless celebrating the Alsatian benefactor of humanity whose bas-relief portrait adorns the base, offering an allegorical mix of candour and obscenity characteristic of *fin-de-siècle* sculptural academicism. Well, this young statue – which I see repeatedly on my walks through the gardens and which still gives me as much pleasure as ever – seemed to me the other day to have changed physically. She seemed to have put on weight; she didn't seem quite so prepubescent and she seemed to have stopped washing: she looked slovenly. Is she perhaps reaching puberty before my very eyes (I am the only person who looks at her)? The mystery of statues, which we presume to be indifferent to their own bodies. This one, as she becomes a woman, will perhaps begin to bleed? Whence perhaps the utility of that strange object she is holding between her slender fingers. And this Doctor 'Kreisler' . . . Was he the inventor of the Tampax, perhaps, or of the dildo?

Cool Memories IV (1995–2000)[13]

New York. Tierra del Fuego

Immediately after: New York. Tierra del Fuego being the distant, peripheral extremity, New York the central extremity, the extreme centre of gravity of our world. Each, in its way, gives the impression of being on another planet. The dilation of geological time on Tierra del Fuego; here its diffraction and acceleration in real time – as timeless in its superficiality as the other in its depth. And if, down there, the sun lies to the north at noon, which always seems so marvellous to a northerner, it seems just as strange that the same sun rises and sets on New York, whose astral theme seems so indifferent to any other orbit but its own. Standing at the tip of Manhattan, towards Ellis and Staten Islands, you are on the banks of the Beagle Channel.

New York

High tension – a perpetual anticyclone: since energy is a form of catastrophe, New York is indeed the epicentre of a catastrophe. The millions of people in the streets seem to have nothing to do but make New York exist – New York having nothing to do but be the centre of the world. It is in this sense that it represents only itself, and everything which happens here has global importance. It is the charm of this city to have turned not just the rest of the United States, but the rest of the world, into an immense province. Hence the foreboding of catastrophe which hovers over the whole city, though it is an exhilarated sense of foreboding, the sense of a collective sacrifice. No social bond, no conviviality, no responsibility to past or future – you don't reproduce in New York. New York isn't a city for reproducing in. Everything produces itself (everything happens) there, and that is that. It is a once-and-for-all city, with no thought for the morrow.

Naples

In its urban incoherence, Naples is the finest example of the fact that the results of absolute disorder are the same as the results of absolute order.

Pompeii

The charm of catastrophe is that it has no equivalent in real time. If we revive it in some form of virtual reality, we destroy it. Yet that is what is being planned today: Euro-Pompeii as a live 'spectacular' with a 'reality show' of the eruption of Vesuvius, etc. Pompeii vitrified, vacuum-sealed, Pompeii buried beneath flows of tourist lava today serves as a bargaining counter for all future catastrophe simulations. The equivalent of the closed, forbidden cave of Lascaux, which serves as archaeological gold reserve and stock exchange.

Disney Company

In the end, the Disney Company will no longer even need to buy up companies or invest. Districts, towns and entire populations will ask to be attached to Disney Unlimited, will themselves request entry to the Fourth Dimension.

Future Cities

Future cities will merely be subsidiaries of the airports, just as current cities are merely terminals for the motorways which crisscross the land.

The future airport will be 75 miles from Paris. Supposing they build it to the north, and Brussels airport is built at the same distance from that city to the south, they will have only to merge the two airports to take us from the one city to the other. There will no longer be any need to take off. Everything will have merged in the same flight area. A single great air terminal for a unified Europe. You will have only to take the secondary connections for Frankfurt, London, Madrid. In other words, things will be exactly as they were before, but inside the European acropolis. Or, even better, a world air terminal. The planet turned into one great air terminal, so that journeys take place, in corrected real time, inside the same network. You could even look at the possibility of getting rid of all the planes, since there would no longer be any point to air traffic.

St Petersburg

All along the walls of the Peter and Paul Fortress, in the first days of spring the sunbathers of perestroika offer themselves up naked – or almost naked – to the sun's exterminating rays. They seem to hang from the red ochre wall, as though thrown against it by some kind of centrifugal force. Like the irradiated silhouettes of Hiroshima, or the skeletons of the Convento dei Cappuccini at Palermo. Or like the Mur des Fusillés or the Wailing Wall, or like the Platonic shadows on the walls of the cave, or those bodies in Signorelli's fresco at Orvieto only half emerging from the earth, covered with a colourless, barely resuscitated flesh – this is what the pale bodies of St Petersburg look like, hardly out of winter limbo yet, freshly dug up and propped there motionless, their eyes closed, men and women all mingled together, like torture victims.

A strange ritual, this show of flesh in the middle of the city, this solar prostitution, which resembles nothing so much as an execution. On the very site where thousands of political prisoners were tortured to death by the Tsars.

Bogotá

On one side, the immense pollution, the immense metropolitan hum of Bogotá rising towards the monastery, towards the Way of the Cross with its copper faces. On the other side of the ridge, the total silence of the equatorial forest.

Buenos Aires

Buenos Aires at six in the morning. At this hour the Avenida de Mayo is the most beautiful in the world, deserted as a landing strip. The lights change from red to green with the same regularity – the only trace of artificial light in the world of early morning. On the road out to the airport, the fields are shrouded in mist, with just the treetops and the advertising hoardings peering out in the horizontal sunlight. Everything is so beautiful like this; the day should end here and now.

Palacio Itamarati

All the gentry of Rio surrounded by the tropical downpour in a palace worthy of Caracalla – the columns of the porticos competing with the fluorescent palms, and the swans on the lake indifferent beneath the deluge. Remake of *The Exterminating Angel*. Thousands of guests at the Biennale, all of them of rare elegance, scattered around the immense halls. The last women arrive, their dresses steaming with rain. The downpour seems to have hit the palace particularly heavily. The other parts of the city have been spared. Is this God's judgement on the usurp-ation for cultural purposes of what was previously a shrine to power?

California

California: the only authentic Disneyland. The only place in the world where the simulacrum is a home-grown product. All the rest is Disneyfied, but Southern California remains the cradle of hyperreality, the capital of nowhere-land.

Villa Palagonia (Palermo)

Surrounded by monsters, gnomes and misshapen figures formed in the image of the Duke of Palagonia who built it and who, being himself deformed and misshapen, to rectify fate's cruel disfavour cunningly covered all the rooms, including the ceilings, with convex or concave mirrors so that everyone appeared deformed or misshapen. This included his wife, who was very beautiful, but whom he could not bear to see pride herself on the fact. So he posted up the following words in the vestibule of the great hall (the residence itself is built in spiral form):

> *Specchiati in quelli cristalli*
> *e nell'istessa*
> *magnificenza singular*
> *contempla*
> *di fralezza mortale*
> *l'immago espressa.*

> Regard yourself in these crystals
> And in this same
> Singular magnificence
> Contemplate
> The express image
> Of a mortal fragility.

Villa Palagonia II

So neither the Villa Palagonia nor the Catacombs of the Cappuccini, with their hundreds of embalmed wraiths standing in their passages, provide us with a sense of death or a mortal fragility. They are simulacra, and they negotiate death by the spectacle of death, death in itself being unimaginable. The – always more or less funereal and melancholy – charm of the simulacrum is that it allows us not to choose between illusion and reality.

The farandole of monsters in the villa's gardens, and the villa itself, are surrounded today, deep in the suburbs of Palermo, by a much worse monstrosity: that of the concrete tower blocks and the frenzy of traffic, of modern sound and fury – the true seventh circle of hell, as Ceronetti would say; the upsurge of a technicity which has wiped from its imagination the very idea of Evil, the principle of Evil, and by comparison with which the space of the villa stands as a last initiatory remnant, preserving in its mirrors, though not for long, the silence of fragility.

True death, annihilation, extermination, is there outside. The pure product of modernity, which, better than any moral value, the spark of Evil still resists.

Notes

1. Extracts reprinted by permission of Verso from paragraphs entitled 'New York', 'Santa Barbara', 'Venice – Porterville', 'Disneyland', 'The Bonaventure Hotel', 'The Realized Utopia' and 'Desert Flower' from J. Baudrillard, *America*, London: Verso, 1990.

2. Extracts reprinted by permission of Verso from J. Baudrillard, *Cool Memories I (1980–85)*, London: Verso, 1997. Translated by Chris Turner.

3. Translated from the French by Sheena Cleland, Wordsmith.

4. In English in original.

5. In English in original.

6. Extracts reprinted by permission of Verso from J. Baudrillard, *Cool Memories II (1987–90)*, London: Verso, 1997. Translated by Chris Turner.

7. Translated from the French by Sheena Cleland, Wordsmith.

8. Translated from the French by Sheena Cleland, Wordsmith.

9. In English in original.

10. This in an allusion to the biblical Arche d'Alliance (the Ark of the Covenant), as well as an ironic reference to the use here being made of the arch at La Défense.

11. Extracts reprinted by permission of Verso from J. Baudrillard, *Cool Memories III (1992–95)*, London: Verso, 1997. Translated by Chris Turner.

12. These are located on the coast of Brittany.

13. Extracts reprinted by permission of Verso from J. Baudrillard, *Cool Memories IV (1995–2000)*, London: Verso, 2003. Translated by Chris Turner.

Chapter Three

THE INDIFFERENCE OF SPACE

Le Parc de la Villette[1]

After the vertical, modern and maximalist hyperrealism of the great cultural ensembles, here we have the horizontal, minimal, conceptual and post-modern hyperrealism of La Villette. Nobody really manages to create a clean sheet, nor to deliver a deconstructed conceptual space, divested of the dead connotations of architecture and of everyday life. Why not leave room for total illusion, why not build a gigantic camera obscura, where we can pass from the other side of the lens (through which we are seen, through which the object sees us), or indeed a gigantic hologram, through which we can pass into the light, having become our own allegory of light, and ourselves become bright corpuscles? On Alice's chessboard, through the looking-glass, anything can happen from one square to another.

The more everyday life is eroded and popularised, and becomes banal and interactive, the more it has to be countered by objects, or by complex and initiatory rules of the game. The more reality (of architecture, of the subject, of everyday life, of art) is reconciled with its concept in a generality with no object, the more we need to make the initial break and seek the power of illusion. If we cannot make the world the object of our desires, we can at least make it the object of a higher convention, which indeed evades our desire (phew!). Every illusion, every initiation is governed by strict rules. Every new object must fulfil all the simultaneous dimensions of the game which made up the raft of Caillois' categories. To find all the dimensions of the game – the aleatory, the vertiginous, the agonic and the allegorical – in a single one. To recompose the spectrum. A work of art, an object, a park, a piece of architecture or anti-architecture, a crime, an event, a journey – they should be an allegory of something, a challenge to someone. They should bring in an element of chance, and give you vertigo.

The initiation resolutely opposes the juxtaposition of things. It is an irreversible course. No one knows where it's leading, but one knows that, no more than in any game, it is not a contract to be negotiated and reconciled – it's a pact. One does not meander around a chessboard the same way one might browse on a computer terminal or stroll around a sports pitch. There is not a post-modern version of chess, or of seduction, or of any other game. Or rather there is exactly that: there is a rash of postmodern games, but they are no longer games of initiation, they are interactive games, tactical or playful games – and that's something else. And perhaps architecture too has become 'something else'; perhaps it has given up the *architectural pact*? Is there an architectural pact? A pact of initiation, which changes the coordinates of reality and illusion, a line beyond which visitors (for example, to Tschumi's park) find themselves initiated into another space, seduced by an object other than their own every-day behaviour (albeit synthesised and multiplied, but what does it matter if the suburbs find a second home here? This summary is condescending: the suburb is an original universe which does not need to be repatriated, it needs no zoological gardens). I would say the same, in a rash and cavalier extrapolation, of the object, of the mass, of the world as such: these are original things which don't need to be justified, repatriated, over-interpreted or staged (especially not by architecture, which above all should take care to be an immanent and irrevocable object).

Fortunately, parks are still made for shadows. What is a park without the shadows circulating within it? Delicious abstractions that tell of the passionate life of the world around them (it's already a long way away), which tell of the passions and pleasures of architecture along the diagonal paths and the cinematic promenades – but they are jealous shadows best avoided.

It's always the same problem: architecture, like teaching or power, tries to fade into the background in order to let unknown truths, social realities and creativity be seen, so that they may come to the fore and express themselves. One puts in place a floating signifier, floating rules of the game, so that sense and acts can flourish freely. Put in place a deconstructed network, a screen of deconstruction which leaves a hypothetical subject the autonomy to invent particular rules of the game. But such rules are never neat, nor are they anyone's property. This is a utopia. One must count on the inevitable reversal of every model, whatever it may be, especially as there are more and more things which are quite simply unimaginable, and they are already there in everyday life, often more solidly and gratifyingly real than in any artistic or imaginary project.

Whatever it may be, no piece of architecture, no project can take into account this distortion, perversion and subtle form of seduction that is the very power of the object. This antagonism can only come from elsewhere, from a blind spot; here from a public too gross to even know what it wants. Plainly, its deconstruction is certainly not the same as that of the programme. And this is not an objection to the programme, as it cannot respond to the opening gambit that plays out at the level of the object and of the enigmatic partnership. The object itself is always a bit like the monster in *Alien* that roams the passages of the spacecraft. It becomes strong, deep down inside, to absorb the bad vibrations.

The ensemble of La Villette cannot be detached from the ensemble of urban monsters that have sprung up in the past or are yet to come. Beaubourg remains their prototype and corresponds to the modern destiny of architecture. That is of course not the intention, but the way things turn out closer to Roissy than to the Louvre even when they are labelled art, culture or museums. They are still at the epicentre of a heavy utopia, a heavy culturalism, which cannot get out of its own shadow.

The park of La Villette seems to portray a lighter utopia, one that is an osmosis of all activities, fulfilling the function of a sort of social chlorophyll. It absorbs toxins, regenerates cells and the ambient air by oxygenation. But it is also an object that does not look out over the city, but has become the city once more, in the sense that it would once again become possible to move there. That's just not possible elsewhere, where we do nothing but go round and round in circles. A place where walking, looking, playing and resting become in themselves 'follies' and fantasy. A recreational space, and not a flow converter. A diverter, not a converter.

One can imagine La Villette and its grounds like a modern, 21st-century cloister. Cloisters and monasteries too encompass whole cities and their activities; yet remain quite distinct from the town and the world. They impose a contemplative stroll, they preserve ordered, 'regular' movement, and they do not open onto secular confusion. They assume the constraints of work and the world, but they are close to the sudden freedom to walk, think and rest that was found in the cloister. La Villette can be seen as a cloister, where its paths are the ambulatory, its follies are the chapels, and its gardens are the diverticulum. A dream . . . of course, on the horizon can be seen the sombre mass of the Museum of Arts and Crafts, the bunker cathedral which already belongs to another reign, that of the clergy, and the end of the cloister; and La Géode, which so resembles a transparent bubble enveloping the vicious demons of Hieronymus Bosch; and La Halle, which has probably seen more blood flow than all the battles of the Middle Ages.

In Beaubourg, the architecture still contains a cultural polysemy, a social apprenticeship to culture. There is still a modern utopia of culture. Even if it is on sale at a massive discount there, it does not yet blend into a pure and simple lifestyle scenario. It is still a mausoleum. But everything leads us to believe that we shall continue to advance inexorably towards a blend of culture and life, towards a denial by culture itself of its distinctive traits, and the many attempts to adapt works of art, architecture in particular, to the social banality of behaviour will always tend in this direction. In this sense, the ensemble of La Villette can appear, in its entirety, like a zoo of everyday life. We no longer seek to create an exceptional object that is unusual, transcendent, that electrifies the imagination. Instead, we create a synoptic anthology of urban walkways and urban living, the epitome of experimental cohabitation.

Here lies the problem. In this inevitable crushing erosion of cultural relief, in this progressive slide towards pure and simple verification of the social, and the indifference of society towards its own culture, what is the destiny of architecture, if it fancies itself as the indecipherable hieroglyphic script of a lust for power that exceeds all social uses? Inventing a public space is indeed a grand design. But what's the point of wanting to recreate it in an enclosed space that is designated and protected (whatever it may be) while the whole problem is that public space is disappearing in the rest of the city? Failing that, why not preserve the idea of public space and open a museum of public space? All the actors and characters are there at La Villette. It's got the ghosts of architecture, of the city, of culture, technology and art, laid out in a more complete and intelligent manner. But where's the drama? We get the impression we're watching repeats of overly tame sequences and special effects in closed circuit stereo. There is too much capillarity, too much osmosis, too many transitions and communicating vessels, too much lubrication and too much interaction. The smallest common denominator of madness and delirium. In reality, in the same way as Los Angeles goes far beyond Disneyland in kitsch novelty, the real devastated spaces are all around in the city and they are far more deconstructed than the Museum of Ideal Deconstruction that they surround. The park and the museum seek to disguise and exorcise the devastation and desertification of the town. But the real picture is that of the devastated city, and the real drama is between that and the Ideal City.

Urbanism and Architecture[2]

Is there such a thing as an architectural pact? A pact of initiation, that which changes the coordinates of reality and illusion, a form by which we will be initiated into another space, seduced by an object other than the urban and functional décor of our everyday behaviour?

In the past, things were threatened by their doubles. Now, in a way, things are threatened by their second homes. Museums are second homes for works of art. Shopping malls and forums are second homes for goods and exchange values. Zoos are second homes for animals. Free spaces are second homes for spontaneity. Erotic chat-rooms are second homes for sexuality. All screens in general are second homes for images and imagination. Has architecture itself not become a second home for space?

That is to say in trying to save an endangered symbolic space, to paper over the cracks in operational urban space, we make it basically a spatial asylum. We guard against the psychosis threatening us all with the mild neurosis of space. The danger is that architecture may be lost as a form and may become a mere spatial therapy.

In its most recent forms, architecture is already becoming transparent, mobile, flexible and interactive. It almost tries to disappear in order to let a hypothetical mass creativity show through. It replaces the immaterial with floating rules of the game, a screen of deconstruction which leaves the subjects quite free to invent their own game rules. Besides, architecture is not the only thing to give way to this interactive utopia of exchange and playful recreation: all art, politics and virtual technology is going in this direction. But the rules of the game do not belong to anyone. Every model, every project must inevitably expect to be thwarted. If the architect is indeed the conceiving subject, he is never master of the city or the masses, nor of the architectural object itself and its use. If you create high cultural definition television, the public will use it in a vulgar and simplistic way. If you give it vulgar television, the public will use it in a complex or casual way. Thus it would be the free subject, the autonomous actor it was supposed to be. The public would seek its autonomy as much in inferiority as in superiority to the model. One is no better than the other, *so there is never any constitutive or deconstructive cultural state*. And there is no reason why any individual or the public should not oppose an intelligent choice just as resolutely as a stupid one. If you install rigid structures, they will invent flexibility. But if you propose flexibility, they will invent something else – just as children do with their toys. That reaction, this malign inflection, this perverse effect cannot be built into any forecast, even those that can accommodate very subtly the technological and philosophical imagination of their time. This turnaround is nothing to do with architectural engineering, it is the effect of the ill will that is engineered behind all objects.

But then on what terrain of new individual and collective desires can an architectural project now open? All spaces have been colonised; not just all geographical spaces but all mental ones too. All phantasms have been sought out, brought back to life and then frozen. The two hemispheres of our brains have been beatified and fossilised in turn. Walt Disney inaugurated an era of infantile paralysis of the imagination, and this virus threatens all enterprises, in that they can no longer be reclaimed from an individual or collective imagination projected onto its own desires. That distortion comes from this floating blind spot, from this very powerlessness of the public to sense what they want; it comes from this subtle way of seducing all projects, this antagonistic power of the object that can only come from elsewhere. The programme, the architectural calculation is always a contract, and it can only fulfil the terms of its contract. But it cannot respond to the symbolic architectural pact – this unfortunate phase where it runs into material things like accidents, resistance, blind denial, ill will, indifference and strong feelings against it. The programme (all programmes: not only architectural ones, but political, cultural and economic programmes) seeks to circumvent this bad part, to distil it in homeopathic doses, even to use it as an inverse energy. It's a necessary illusion. But can the bad part have its own architecture? Architecture cannot just seek to be an ideal allegory of the city, it cannot conceptualise the bad part. This is what takes over architecture despite itself, and makes its products monstrosities – literally unidentifiable objects, experimental *coups de théâtre* in a city itself devoted to the theme of town planning.

Architecture in its ambitious form no longer builds anything but monsters, in that they no longer testify to the integrity of a town, but to its disintegration; not to its organic nature, but to its disorganisation. They do not give rhythm to the town and its exchanges, they are dumped on it like space debris 'fallen from some unknown disaster'. Neither central nor peripheral, they describe a false centrality and around them a false sphere of influence. In reality, they bear witness to the satellisation of urban existence. Their attraction is the way in which tourists are amazed and their function, like interchanges in general (airports, motorways, hypermarkets) is as a place of expulsion, extradition and urban ecstasy. Furthermore, Beaubourg remains the prototype of this modern architectural destiny, which marginal groups and subculture come looking for above all: an empty ecstasy, a cosmopolitan strike, something to leech off.

Beaubourg, but also La Défense, the Forum and La Villette: these are no longer influential or contemplative objects, but places of absorption and excretion, flow converters, input-output devices (gigantic celibate machines, no longer lustful!). They seem less emanations and evocations of the city than refugees from a universal exhibition, witnesses to the cosmopolitan and unmeasured movement of our societies.

On this note I would like to recall a good example from about ten years ago – the cleaning strike at Beaubourg. This strike, the revenge of the little people, quickly transformed the cultural space of Beaubourg into a gigantic rubbish space. Now at that very time there was an exhibition taking place on waste. You might say that the Centre the strikers transformed into an accidental dumping ground went far beyond the banal exhibition on show inside as a demonstration object. Of course nobody dared say that it was the strike that was the real cultural performance and the strikers the Centre's real artists – but they were, because they alone illustrated the prevailing cultural state of the city.

Such is the current pathology of architecture. But, paradoxically, such is also the original effect of these kinds of extraterrestrial objects that telescope the city in an unforeseen manner. Because ultimately, it is perhaps a good thing that all the intentions underlying the Beaubourg project were contradicted by the object. There is a sort of revenge to it. Based on a positive outlook (culture, participation, communication), in the end the project was completely crossed by the reality, indeed hyperreality of the object. Instead of being contextual, it created empty space around itself and became a sort of black body. With its flexible, unqualitative, dispersed spaces and its transparency, it was supposed to be in step with modern culture. In fact, it ran into an accumulation which, by its massive response, came to obscure all these intentions. The object no longer fulfils its objective; contradiction came savagely into play. Thus the object (both the building and the mass) has an inhumanity that contradicts all the project's humanist intentions. This reversal will have been a sort of destiny for Beaubourg. And no architecture can hope to evade it. Perhaps we should rather exploit this surprise; rediscover this paradox, this enigma, this radical surprise that can only come from the object?

Koolhaas's book (*Delirious New York*) contained a very good idea in this regard: it was a vision of the Coney Island theme park as an architectural project for Manhattan – a kind of super-production that had become the apex of architecture (or anti-architecture). It is the precession of the object over the project: something happened there that passed the architects by. Thus, an ultimately admirable architecture was built on foundations that were *a priori* atrocious and inhuman. The object needs to escape from its creator to become brilliant in itself and reach out to users. This is the price of architecture escaping from functional indifference.

> We are all gamblers. What we desire most intensely is that
> the inexorable procession of rational connection cease for a
> while. That there be installed, even for a short time, an
> unheard-of unravelling of another kind, a marvellous
> escalation of events, an extraordinary succession, as if
> predestined, of the smallest details, to the point where we
> think that things – until now maintained artificially at a
> distance through a contract of succession and causality –
> suddenly find themselves, not delivered over to chance, but
> converging spontaneously, concurring through their very
> connection in this self-same intensity.[3]

Everything is round in the end. The earth is round and, in the world of imagination, there should also be an inevitable curvature which resists all flattening, all linearity, all programming.

Another effect of the monstrosity of these super-objects, of these object-models, is that the city and the whole urban context become remnants and waste products. That is the result of the global enterprise of ideal programming, of artificial modelling of the world, the specialisation and centralisation of functions that the modern metropolis obviously symbolises, and of the world-wide extension of these artificial ensembles. In producing these model cities, these model functions, we make all the rest waste, residue, a useless vestige. If you build a motorway, supermarket or supercity, you automatically make everything around it into desert. If you create ultra-fast automatic networks, or fixed circulation, you immediately make all traditional exchange space a deserted area. The same is true of motorways, which create a desert of land around them. It will be the same with the information superhighway, which will result in a future desert, a communications sub-underworld of all the informatically excluded and exiled, to say nothing of the mental desert made of all the brains put out of technical work by artificial intelligence networks. On a far grander scale, these will be the descendants of the exiles from the world of work who are today's millions of unemployed.

Note

1. Translated from the French by Sheena Cleland, Wordsmith.
2. Translated from the French by Sheena Cleland, Wordsmith.
3. Jean Baudrillard, *Fatal Strategies*, London: Pluto, 1990, p 153.

Chapter Four

THE CODE AND THE EYE

Simulations[1]

Hyperreal and imaginary

Disneyland is a perfect model of all the entangled orders of simulation. To begin with it is a play of illusion and phantasms: Pirates, the Frontier, Future World, etc. This imaginary world is supposed to be what makes the operation successful. But what draws the crowds is undoubtedly much more the social microcosm, the miniaturised and *religious* revelling in real America, in its delights and drawbacks. You park outside, queue up inside, and are totally abandoned at the exit. In this imaginary world the only phantasmagoria is in the inherent warmth and affection of the crowd, and in that sufficiently excessive number of gadgets used there to specifically maintain the multitudinous affect. The contrast with the absolute solitude of the parking lot – a veritable concentration camp – is total. Or rather: inside, a whole range of gadgets magnetise the crowd into direct flows – outside, solitude is directed onto a single gadget: the automobile. By an extraordinary coincidence (one that undoubtedly belongs to the peculiar enchantment of this universe), this deep-frozen infantile world happens to have been conceived and realised by a man who is himself now cryogenised: Walt Disney, who awaits his resurrection at minus 180° centigrade.

The objective profile of America, then, may be traced throughout Disneyland, even down to the morphology of individuals and the crowd. All its values are exalted here, in miniature and comic strip form. Embalmed and pacified. Whence the possibility of an ideological analysis of Disneyland (L. Marin does it well in *Utopies, jeux d'espaces*): digest of the American way of life, panegyric to American values, idealised transposition of a contradictory reality. To be sure. But this conceals something else, and that 'ideological' blanket exactly serves to cover over a *third-order simulation*: Disneyland is there to conceal the fact that it is the 'real' country, all of 'real' America, which *is* Disneyland (just as prisons are there to conceal the fact that it is the social in its entirety, in its banal omnipresence, which is carceral). Disneyland is presented as imaginary in order to make us believe that the rest is real, when in fact all of Los Angeles and the America surrounding it are no longer real, but of the order of the hyperreal and of simulation. It is no longer a question of a false representation of reality (ideology), but of concealing the fact that the real is no longer real, and thus of saving the reality principle.

The Disneyland imaginary is neither true nor false; it is a deterrence machine set up in order to rejuvenate in reverse the fiction of the real. Whence the debility, the infantile degeneration of this imaginary. It is meant to be an infantile world, in order to make us believe that the adults are elsewhere, in the 'real' world, and to conceal the fact that real childishness is everywhere, particularly amongst those adults who go there to act the child in order to foster illusions as to their real childishness.

Moreover, Disneyland is not the only one. Enchanted Village, Magic Mountain, Marine World: Los Angeles is encircled by these 'imaginary stations' which feed reality, reality-energy, to a town whose mystery is precisely that it is nothing more than a network of endless, unreal circulation – a town of fabulous proportions, but without space or dimensions. As much as electrical and nuclear power stations, as much as film studios, this town, which is nothing more than an immense script and a perpetual motion picture, needs this old imaginary made up of childhood signals and faked phantasms for its sympathetic nervous system.

The stucco angel

It is in the Renaissance that the false is born along with the natural. From the fake shirt in front to the use of the fork as artificial prosthesis, to the stucco interiors and the great baroque theatrical machinery. The entire classical era belongs *par excellence* to the theatre. Theatre is the form which takes over social life and all of architecture from the Renaissance on. It's there, in the prowess of stucco and baroque art, that you read the metaphysic of the counterfeit and the new ambitions of Renaissance man – those of a *worldly demiurge*, a transubstantiation of all of nature into a unique substance, theatrical like social life unified under the sign of bourgeois values, beyond all differences in blood, rank, or of caste. Stucco means democracy triumphant over all artificial signs, the apotheosis of theatre and fashion, and it betrays the new class's infinite capabilities, its power to do anything once it has been able to break through the exclusiveness of signs. The way lies open to unheard-of combinations, to all the games all the counterfeits – the Promethean verve of the bourgeoisie first plunged into the *imitation of nature* before throwing itself into *production*. In the churches and palaces stucco is wed to all forms, imitates everything – velvet curtains, wooden corniches, carnal swelling of the flesh. Stucco exorcizes the unlikely confusion of matter into a single new substance, a sort of general equivalent of all the others, and is prestigious theatrically because it is itself a representative substance, a mirror of all the others.

But simulacra are not only a game played with signs; they imply social rapports and social power. Stucco can come off as the exaltation of a rising science and technology; it is also connected to the baroque which in turn is tied to the enterprise of the Counter Reformation and the hegemony over the political and mental world that the Jesuits – who were the first to act according to modern conceptions of power – attempted to establish.

There is a strict correlation between the mental obedience of the Jesuits (*'perinde ac cadaver'*) and the demiurgic ambition to exorcize the natural substance of a thing in order to substitute a synthetic one. Just like a man submitting his will to his organization, things take on the ideal functionality of the cadaver. All technology, all technocracy are incipiently there: the presumption of an ideal counterfeit of the world, expressed in the invention of a universal substance and of a universal amalgam of substances. Reunify the scattered world (after the Reformation) under the aegis of a homogeneous doctrine, universalize the world under a single word (from New Spain to Japan: the Missions), constitute a political elite *of the state*, with an identically centralized strategy: these are the objectives of the Jesuits. In order to accomplish this, you need to create effective simulacra: the apparatus of the organization is one, but also its clerkly magnificence and the theatre (the great theatre of the cardinals and grey eminences). And training and education are other simulacra that aimed, for the first time ever in a systematic manner, at remodelling an ideal nature from a child. That architectural sauce of stucco and baroque is a great apparatus of the same kind. All of the above precedes the productivist rationality of capital, but everything testifies already – not in production, but in counterfeit to the same project of control and universal hegemony – to a social scheme where the internal coherence of a system is already at work.

Once there lived in the Ardennes an old cook, to whom the molding of buildings out of cakes and the science of plastic patisserie had given the ambition to take up the creation of the world where God had left it, in its natural phase, so as to eliminate organic spontaneity and substitute for it a single, unique and polymorphous matter: Reinforced Concrete: concrete furniture, chairs, drawers, concrete sewing machines, and outside in the courtyard, an entire orchestra, including violins, of concrete – all concrete! Concrete trees with real leaves printed into them, a hog made out of real reinforced concrete, but with a real hog's skull inside, concrete sheep covered with real wool. Camille Renault had finally found the original substance, the paste from which different things can only be distinguished by 'realistic' nuance: the hog's skull, leaves of the tree – but this was doubtless only a concession of the demiurge to his visitors . . . for it was with an adorable smile that this 80-year-old god received visitors to his creation. He sought no argument with divine creation; he was remaking it only to render it more intelligible. Nothing here of a Luciferan revolt, or a will-to-parody, or of a desire to espouse the cause of naive art. The Ardennes cook reigned simply over a unified mental substance (for concrete is a *mental* substance; it allows, just like a concept, phenomena to be organized and divided up at will). His project was not so far from that of the builders in stucco of baroque art, nor very different from the projection on the terrain of an urban community in the current great ensembles. The counterfeit is working, so far, only on substance and form, not yet on relations and structures. But it is aiming already, on this level, at the control of a pacified society, ground up into a synthetic, deathless substance: an indestructible artifact that will guarantee an eternity of power. Is it not man's miracle to have invented, with plastic, a non-degradable material, interrupting thus the cycle which, by corruption and death, turns all the earth's substances ceaselessly one into another? A substance out-of-the-cycle; even fire leaves an indestructible residue. There is something incredible about it, this simulacrum where you can see in a condensed form the universal semiotic. This has nothing to do with the 'progress' of technology or with a rational goal for science. It is a project of political and cultural hegemony, the fantasy of a closed mental substance – like those angels of baroque stucco whose extremities meet in a curved mirror.

The tactile and the digital

From the smallest disjunctive unit (question/answer particle) up to the great alternating systems that control the economy, politics, world co-existence, the matrix does not change: it is always the 0/1, the binary scansion that is affirmed as the metastable or homeostatic for the current systems. This is the nucleus of the simulation processes which dominate us. It can be organized as a play of unstable variations, from polyvalence to tautology, without threatening the strategic bipolar form: it is the divine of simulation.

Why are there *two* towers at New York's World Trade Center? All of Manhattan's great buildings were happy enough to affront each other in a competitive verticality, the result of which is an architectural panorama the image of the capitalist system: a pyramidal jungle, all the buildings attacking each other. The system profiled itself in a celebrated image that you had of New York when you arrived there by boat. This image has completely changed in the last few years. The effigy of the capitalist system has passed from the pyramid to the perforated card. Buildings are no longer obelisks, but lean one upon the other, no longer suspicious one of the other, like columns in a statistical graph. This new architecture incarnates a system that is no longer competitive, but compatible, and where competition has disappeared for the benefit of the correlations. (New York is the world's only city therefore that retraces all along its history, and with prodigious fidelity and in all its scope, the actual form of the capitalistic system – it changes instantly in function of the latter. No European city does so.) This architectural graphism is that of the monopoly; the two WTC towers, perfect parallelepipeds a 1/4-mile high on a square base, perfectly balanced and blind communicating vessels. The fact that there are two of them *signifies* the end of all competition, the end of all original reference. Paradoxically, if there were only one, the monopoly would not be incarnated, because we have seen how it stabilizes on a dual form. For the sign to be pure, it has to duplicate itself: it is the duplication of the sign which destroys its meaning. This is what Andy Warhol demonstrates also: the multiple replicas of Marilyn's face are there to show at the same time the death of the original and the end of representation. The two towers of the WTC are the visible sign of the closure of the system in a vertigo of duplication, while the other skyscrapers are each of them the original moment of a system constantly transcending itself in a perpetual crisis and self-challenge.

There is a particular fascination in this reduplication. As high as they are, higher than all the others, the two towers signify nevertheless the end of verticality. They ignore the other buildings, they are not of the same race, they no longer challenge them, nor compare themselves to them, they look one into the other as into a mirror and culminate in this prestige of similitude. What they project is the idea of the model that they are one for the other, and their twin altitude presents no longer any value of transcendence. They signify only that the strategy of models and commutations wins out in the very heart of the system itself – and New York is really the heart of it – over the traditional strategy of competition. The buildings of Rockefeller Center still direct their gaze one at the other into their glass or steel facades, in the city's infinite specularity. The towers, on the other hand, are blind, and no longer have a facade. All referential of habitat, of the facade as face, of interior and exterior, that you still find in the Chase

Manhattan or in the boldest mirror-buildings of the '60s, is erased. At the same time as the rhetoric of verticality, the rhetoric of the mirror has disappeared. There remains only a series closed on the number two, just as if architecture, in the image of the system, proceeded only from a unchangeable genetic code, a definitive model.

Trompe l'Oeil or Enchanted Simulation [2]

Disenchanted simulation: pornography – truer than true – the height of the simulacrum.

Enchanted simulation: the *trompe l'oeil* – falser than false – the secret of appearances.

Neither fable, story or composition, nor theater, scene or action. The *trompe l'oeil* forgets all this and bypasses it by the low-level representation of second-rate objects. The latter figure in the great compositions of the time, but here they appear alone, as though the discourse on painting had been eliminated. Suddenly they no longer 'represent,' they are no longer objects, no longer anything. They are blank, empty signs that bespeak a social, religious or artistic anti-ceremony or anti-representation. Scraps of social life, they turn against the latter and parody its theatricality; this is why they are scattered, juxtaposed at random. The implication being that *these objects are not objects*. They do not describe a familiar reality, as does a still life. They describe a void, an absence, the absence of every representational hierarchy that organizes the elements of a tableau, or for that matter, the political order . . .

These are not mere extras displaced from the main scene, but ghosts that haunt the emptiness of the stage. Theirs is not the aesthetic appeal of painting and resemblance, but the acute, metaphysical appeal of the real's abolition. Haunted objects, metaphysical objects, in their unreal reversion they are opposed to the entire representative space of the Renaissance.

Their very insignificance is offensive. Objects without referents, stripped of their decor – old newspapers, books, nails, boards, and scraps of food – isolated, decayed, spectral objects, disincarnated from all narrative, they alone were able to trace an obsession with a lost reality, something akin to life before the subject and his acquisition of consciousness. 'For the transparent, allusive image that the art lover expects, the *trompe l'oeil* tends to substitute the intractable opacity of Presence' (Pierre Charpentrat). Simulacra without perspective, the figures in *trompe l'oeil* appear suddenly, with lustrous exactitude, as though denuded of the aura of meaning and bathed in ether. Pure appearances, they have the irony of too much reality.

There is no nature in the *trompe l'oeil*, nor landscapes, skies, vanishing points or natural light. Nor faces, psychology or historicity. Everything is artifact. A vertical backdrop raises objects isolated from their referential context to the status of pure signs.

Translucency, suspense, fragility, obsolescence – hence the insistence on paper (frayed at the edges), the letter, the mirror or watch, the faded, untimely signs of a transcendence that has vanished into the quotidian. The mirror of worn-out boards whose knots and rings mark the time, like a clock without hands that leaves one to guess the hour: these are things that have lasted, in a time that has already passed. Anachrony alone stands out, the involuted representation of time and space.

There are no fruits, meats or flowers, no baskets or bouquets, nor any of the delightful things found in (a still) life. Nature is carnal, and a still life is a carnal arrangement on a horizontal plane, that provided by the ground or a table. Although a still life may sometimes play with disorder, with the ragged edge of things and the fragility of their use, it always retains the gravity of real things, as underscored by the horizontalness. Whereas the *trompe l'oeil* functions in weightlessness, as indicated by the vertical backdrop, everything being suspended, the objects, time, even light and perspective. While the still life uses classic shapes and shades, the shadows borne by the *trompe l'oeil* lack the depth that comes from a *real* luminous source. Like the obsolescence of objects, they are the sign of a slight vertigo, the vertigo of a previous life, of an appearance prior to reality.

This mysterious light without origin, whose oblique rays are no longer real, is like stagnant water, water without depth, soft to the touch like a natural death. Here things have long since lost their shadows (their substance). Something other than the sun shines on them, a brighter star, without an atmosphere, or with an ether that doesn't refract. Perhaps death illuminates these things directly, and that is their sole meaning? These shadows do not move with the sun; they do not grow with the evening; without movement, they appear as an inevitable edging. Not the result of chiaroscuro nor a skilful dialectic of light and shadow (for these are still painterly effects), they suggest the transparency of objects to a black sun.

One senses that these objects are approaching the black hole from which, for us, reality, the real world, and normal time emerge. With this forward decentering effect, this advance towards the subject of a mirror object, it is the appearance of the double, in the guise of trivial objects, that creates the effect of seduction, the startling impression characteristic of the *trompe l'oeil*: a tactile vertigo that recounts the subject's insane desire to obliterate his own image, and thereby vanish. For reality grips us only when we lose ourselves in it, or when it reappears as our own, hallucinated death.

A vague physical wish to grasp things, but which having been suspended, becomes metaphysical: the objects of the *trompe l'oeil* have something of the same fantastic vivacity as the child's discovery of his own image, an unmediated hallucination anterior to the perceptual order.

If there is a miracle of *trompe l'oeil*, it does not lie in the realism of its execution, like the grapes of Zeuxis which appeared so real that birds came to peck at them. This is absurd. Miracles never result from a surplus of reality but, on the contrary, from a sudden break in reality and the giddiness of feeling oneself fall. It is this loss of reality that the *surreal* familiarity of objects translates. With the disintegration of this hierarchical organization of space that privileges the eye and vision, of this perspectival simulation – for it is merely a simulacrum –

something emerges that, for want of something better, we express in terms of *touch*, a tactile hyperpresence of things, 'as though one could hold them.' But this tactile fantasy has nothing to do with our sense of touch; it is a metaphor for the 'seizure' resulting from the annihilation of the scene and space of representation. Suddenly this seizure rebounds onto the so-called 'real' world, to reveal that this 'reality' is naught but a staged world, objectified in accord with the rules of perspective. 'Reality' appears as a *principle*, one that defines the painting, sculpture and architecture of the period, but a principle nonetheless – that is, a simulacrum which the experimental hypersimulation of the *trompe l'oeil* undermines.

The *trompe l'oeil* does not seek to confuse itself with the real. Consciously produced by means of play and artifice, it presents itself as a simulacrum. By mimicking the third dimension, it questions the reality of this dimension, and by mimicking and exceeding the effects of the real, it radically questions the reality principle.

The real is relinquished *by the very excess of its appearances*. The objects resemble themselves too much, this resemblance being like a second state; and by virtue of this *allegorical* resemblance, and of the diagonal lighting, they point to the irony of too much reality.

Depth appears to have been turned inside out. While the Renaissance organized all space in accord with a distant vanishing point, perspective in the *trompe l'oeil* is, in a sense, projected forward. Instead of fleeing before the panoramic sweep of the eye (the privilege of panoptic vision), the objects 'fool' the eye ('*trompent l'oeil*') by a sort of internal depth – not by causing one to believe in a world that does not exist, but by undermining the privileged position of the gaze. The eye, instead of generating a space that spreads out, is but the internal vanishing point for a convergence of objects. A different universe occupies the foreground, a universe without horizon or horizontality, like an opaque mirror placed before the eye, with nothing behind it. This is, properly speaking, the realm of appearances, where there is nothing to see, where things see you.

They do not flee before your gaze, but position themselves in front of you, with a light that seems to come from another world, with shadows that never quite give them a true third dimension. For this dimension, that of perspective, always indicates the bad conscience of the sign relative to reality – a bad conscience that has eaten away at all painting since the Renaissance.

Whence independent of the aesthetic pleasure, comes the uncanniness of the *trompe l'oeil* – the strange light it casts on this entirely new, Western reality which emerged triumphant with the Renaissance. The *trompe l'oeil* is the *ironic simulacrum* of that reality. It is what surrealism was to the functionalist revolution of the early twentieth century – surrealism being but an ironic reverie on the principle of functionality. And like *trompe l'oeil* surrealism is not quite part of art or art history, for their concern is with a metaphysical dimension, and not with matters of style. They attack our sense of reality or functionality and, therefore, our sense of consciousness. They seek out the wrong or reverse side of things, and undermine the world's apparent factuality. This is why the pleasure that they give us, their seductiveness, however small, is radical; for it comes from a radical surprise borne of appearances, from a life prior to the mode of production of the real world.

The *trompe l'oeil* is no longer confined to painting. Like stucco, its contemporary, it can do anything, mimic or parody anything. It has become the prototype for the malevolent use of appearances. What began as a game took on fantastic dimensions in the sixteenth century, and ended up eliminating the boundaries between painting, sculpture and architecture. In the murals and ceiling paintings of the Renaissance and Baroque, painting and sculpture converge. In the *trompe l'oeil* murals and streets of Los Angeles, architecture is deceived and defaced by illusion. The seduction of space by the signs of space. Having said so much about the production of space, is it not time to speak about its seduction?

And about the seduction of political space. For example, the studiolos of the Duke of Urbino and Federico da Montefeltre in the ducal palace of Urbino and Gubbio: tiny sanctuaries entirely in *trompe l'oeil* at the heart of the immense space of the palace. The latter exemplifies the triumph of an architectural perspective, of a space deployed according to the rules, while the studiolo appears as an inverted microcosm. Cut off from the rest of the structure, without windows, literally without space – *here space is actualized by simulation.* If the palace as a whole constitutes the architectural act *par excellence*, the manifest discourse of art (and power), then what is one to make of the minuscule studiolo that adjoins the chapel like yet another sacred place, but with an air of bewitchment? It is not clear what is happening with regard to space, and consequently, to the entire system of representations that gives order to the palace and republic.

It is a *privatissime* space, the prerogative of the Prince, like incest and transgression were once kingly prerogatives. A complete reversal of the rules of the game is in effect here, allowing us to surmise ironically, by the allegory of the *trompe l'oeil*, that the external space, that of the palace, and beyond it, the city, that is, the political space, the locus of power, *is itself perhaps only an effect of perspective.* Such a dangerous secret, such a radical hypothesis, the Prince must keep to himself in the strictest secrecy: *for it is the very secret of his power.*

Since Machiavelli, politicians have perhaps always known that the mastery of a *simulated* space is at the source of their power, that politics is not a *real* activity, but a simulation model, whose manifest acts are but actualized impressions. It is this blind spot within the palace, cut off from architecture and public life, which in a sense reigns supreme, not by direct determination, but by a sort of internal reversion, by an abrogation of the rules enacted in secret, as in primitive rituals. A hole in reality, an ironic transfiguration, an exact simulacrum hidden at the heart of reality, and on which the latter depends for its functioning. *This is the secret of appearances.*

Thus the Pope, the Grand Inquisitor, the great Jesuits and theologians all knew that God did not exist; this was their secret, and the secret of their strength. Similarly Montefeltre's studiolo in *trompe l'oeil* secretly suggests that, in the last instance, reality does not exist, that 'real' in-depth space, including political space, is always potentially reversible – the secret that once commanded politics, but which has since been lost in the illusion of the masses' 'reality.'

Ecstasy and Inertia[3]

Everything in this city is metaphysical, including its dream-like geometry, not a geometry of space, but a mental geometry, one of labyrinths – the freezing of time even more poignant in the midday heat.

The tactile presence of these ruins, their suspense, their revolving shadows, their everydayness, is magnificent for the psyche. It is the conjunction of the banality of a stroll and the immanence of another time, of another instant, unique, a time of catastrophe. The deadly, but extinguished, presence of Vesuvius gives the deserted streets the charm of a hallucination – the illusion of being here and now, on the verge of eruption – and it is resuscitated, by a miracle of nostalgia, two thousand years later in the immanence of a previous life.

Few places leave such an impression of strange disturbance (it is no surprise that Jansen and Freud have located here the psychic function of Gradiva). It is the very warmth of death that we sense here, brought to life in the fossilized and fugitive signs of everyday existence: wheel tracks in the rock; the signs of wear in the curb; the petrified wood of a half opened door; the pleat of a toga on a body buried in ashes. No history, like the one which gives prestige to monuments, can intervene between these things and ourselves. They are materialized here, at once, in the very heat where death seized them.

Neither monumentality nor beauty is essential to Pompeii – as are the fatal intimacy of things and the fascination in their simultaneity, like the perfect simulacrum of our own death.

Pompeii is a sort of *trompe l'oeil*, a sort of primitive scene: the same vertigo with one dimension missing: time; the same hallucination with an added dimension: the transparency of the smallest detail, like the clear vision of trees completely submerged at the bottom of an artificial lake, which you glide over in your stride. This is the mental effect of catastrophe: stopping things before they come to an end, and holding them suspended in their apparition.

Pompeii again destroyed by an earthquake. What kind of catastrophe so unrelentlessly pursues ruins? What is a ruin that needs to be demolished and buried again? The sadistic irony of catastrophe is that it secretly awaits for things, even ruins, to regain their beauty and meaning only to destroy them once again. It is intent upon destroying the illusion of eternity, but it also plays with that illusion, since it fixates things in an alternate eternity. This fixation-paralysis, the shattering of a presence swarming with life in a catastrophic instant, is what gave Pompeii its charm. The first catastrophe, Vesuvius, was a success. The last seismic movement is much more problematic. It appears to obey the rule of the doubling of events in an effect of parody: the pathetic repetition of the great original. The accomplishment of a great destiny with a little help from a wretched divinity. But it has perhaps another meaning; it comes as a warning that this is no longer the era of great collapses, of resurrections, or of games of death and eternity, but the era of little fractionized events, of smooth and effective annihilation, by progressive slippage, an era henceforth without a future, since the traces themselves erase this new destiny. This inaugurates the horizontal era of events without consequences; the last act was staged by nature itself in a glimmer of parody.

Notes

1.   Extracts reprinted by permission of Semiotext(e) from paragraphs entitled 'Hyperreal and Imaginary', 'The Stucco Angel' and 'The Tactile and The Digital' from J. Baudrillard, *Simulations*, New York: Semiotext(e), 1983.

2.   Extracts reprinted by permission of Palgrave Macmillan from J. Baudrillard, *Seduction*, Basingstoke: Macmillan Education, 1990. Tr. by Brian Singer.

3.   Extracts reprinted by permission of Semiotext(e) from J. Baudrillard, *Fatal Strategies*, New York: Semiotext(e), 1990. Tr. by Philip Beitchman and WGJ Niesluchowski. Edited by Jim Fleming.

Chapter Five

THE RISE OF THE OBJECT:
THE END OF CULTURE

The Formal Liturgy of the Object[1]

The consumer society

Today, we are everywhere surrounded by the remarkable conspicuousness of consumption and affluence, established by the multiplication of objects,
services, and material goods. This now constitutes a fundamental mutation in the
ecology of the human species. Strictly speaking, men of wealth are no longer
surrounded by other human beings, as they have been in the past, but by *objects*.
Their daily exchange is no longer with their fellows, but rather, statistically as a
function of some ascending curve, with the acquisition and manipulation of goods
and messages: from the rather complex domestic organization with its dozens of
technical slaves to the 'urban estate' with all the material machinery of communication and professional activity, and the permanent festive celebration of objects
in advertising with the hundreds of daily mass media messages; from the proliferation of somewhat obsessional objects to the symbolic psychodrama which fuels
the nocturnal objects that come to haunt us even in our dreams. The concepts of
'environment' and 'ambiance' have undoubtedly become fashionable only since
we have come to live in less proximity to other human beings, in their presence

and discourse, and more under the silent gaze of deceptive and obedient objects which continuously repeat the same discourse, that of our stupefied (*medusée*) power, of our potential affluence and of our absence from one another.

As the wolf-child becomes wolf by living among them, so are we becoming functional. We are living the period of the objects: that is we live by their rhythm, according to their incessant cycles. Today, it is we who are observing their birth, fulfilment, and death; whereas in all previous civilizations, it was the object, instrument, and perennial monument that survived the generations of men.

While objects are neither flora nor fauna, they give the impression of being a proliferating vegetation; a jungle where the new savage of modern times has trouble finding the reflexes of civilization. These fauna and flora, which people have produced, have come to encircle and invest them, like a bad science fiction novel. We must quickly describe them as we see and experience them, while not forgetting, even in periods of scarcity or profusion, that they are in actuality the *products of human activity*, and are controlled, not by natural ecological laws, but by the law of exchange value.

> The busiest streets of London are crowded with shops whose show cases display all the riches of the world: Indian shawls, American revolvers, Chinese porcelain, Parisian corsets, furs from Russia and spices from the tropics; but all of these worldly things bear odious white paper labels with Arabic numerals and then laconic symbols £SD. This is how commodities are presented in circulation.

Profusion and display

Accumulation, or *profusion*, is evidently the most striking descriptive feature. Large department stores, with their luxuriant abundance of canned goods, foods, and clothing, are like the primary landscape and the geometrical locus of affluence. Streets with overcrowded and glittering store windows (lighting being the least rare commodity, without which merchandise would merely be what it is), the displays of delicacies, and all the scenes of alimentary and vestimentary festivity, stipulate a magical salivation. Accumulation is more than the sum of its products: the conspicuousness of surplus, the final and magical negation of scarcity, and the maternal and luxurious presumptions of the land of milk and honey. Our markets, our shopping avenues and malls mimic a new-found nature of prodigious fecundity. Those are our Valleys of Canaan where flows, instead of milk and honey, streams of neon on ketchup and plastic – but no matter! There exists an anxious anticipation, not that there may not be enough, but that there is too much, and too much for everyone: by purchasing a portion one in effect appropriates a whole crumbling pyramid of oysters, meats, pears or canned asparagus. One purchases the part for the whole. And this repetitive and metonymic discourse of the consumable, and of commodities is represented, through collective metaphor and as a product of its own surplus, in the image of the *gift*, and of the inexhaustible and spectacular prodigality of the *feast*.

In addition to the stack, which is the most rudimentary yet effective form of accumulation, objects are organized in *displays*, or in *collections*. Almost every clothing store or appliance store presents a gamut of differentiated objects, which call upon, respond to, and refute each other. The display window of the antique store is the aristocratic, luxurious version of this model. The display no longer exhibits an overabundance of wealth but a *range* of select and complementary objects which are offered for the choosing. But this arrangement also invokes a psychological chain reaction in the consumer who peruses it, inventories it, and grasps it as a total category. Few objects today are offered *alone*, without a context of objects to speak for them. And the relation of the consumer to the object has consequently changed: the object is no longer referred to in relation to a specific utility, but as a collection of objects in their total meaning. Washing machine, refrigerator, dishwasher, have different meanings when grouped together than each one has alone, as a piece of equipment (*ustensile*). The display window, the advertisement, the manufacturer, and the *brand name* here play an essential role in imposing a coherent and collective vision, like an almost inseparable totality. Like a chain that connects not ordinary objects but *signifieds*, each object can signify the other in a more complex super-object, and lead the consumer to a series of more complex choices. We can observe that objects are never offered for consumption in an absolute disarray. In certain cases they can *mimic* disorder to better seduce, but they are always arranged to trace out directive paths. The arrangement directs the purchasing impulse towards *networks* of objects in order to seduce it and elicit, in accordance with its own logic, a maximal investment, reaching the limits of economic potential. Clothing, appliances, and toiletries thus constitute object *paths*, which establish inertial constraints on the consumer who will proceed *logically* from one object to the next. The consumer will be caught up in a *calculus* of objects, which is quite different from the frenzy of purchasing and possession which arises from the simple profusion of commodities.

The drugstore

The drugstore is the synthesis of profusion and calculation. The drugstore (or the new shopping malls) makes possible the synthesis of all consumer activities, not least of which are shopping, flirting with objects, idle wandering, and all the permutations of these. In this way, the drugstore is more appropriately representative of modern consumption than the large department store where quantitative centralization leaves little margin for idle exploration. The arrangement of departments and products here imposes a more utilitarian approach to consumption. It retains something of the period of the emergence of department stores, when large numbers of people were beginning to get access to *everyday* consumables. The drugstore has an altogether different function. It does not juxtapose categories of commodities, but practices an *amalgamation of signs* where all categories of goods are considered a partial field in a general consumerism of signs. The cultural center becomes, then, an integral part of the shopping mall. This is not to say that culture is here 'prostituted'; that is too simple. It is *culturalized*. Consequently, the commodity (clothing, food, restaurant, etc.) is also culturalized, since it is transformed into a distinctive and idle substance, a luxury and an item, among others, in the general display of consumables.

A new art of living, a new way of living, claims advertising,
(and fashionable magazines): a pleasant shopping experience,

in a single air-conditioned location; one is able to purchase
food, products for the apartment or summer home, clothing,
flowers, the latest novel, or the latest gadget in a single trip,
while husband and children watch a film; and then later you
can all dine together on the spot.

Café, cinema, book store, auditorium, trinkets, clothing, and many other
things can be found in these shopping centers. The drugstore recaptures it all in
a kaleidoscopic mode. Whereas the large department store provides a market-
place pageantry for merchandise, the drugstore offers the subtle recital of consumption, where, in fact, the 'art' consists in playing on the ambiguity of the
object's sign and sublimating their status and utility as commodity in a play of
'ambiance.'

The drugstore is neo-culture universalized, where there is no longer any
difference between a fine gourmet shop and a gallery of paintings, between
Playboy and a *Treatise on Paleontology*. The drugstore will be modernized to the
point of offering a bit of 'gray matter':

Just selling products does not interest us, we would like to
supply a little gray matter . . . Three stories, a bar, a dance
floor, and shops; trinkets, records, paperbacks, intellectual
books, a bit of everything. But we are not looking to flatter the
customer. We are actually offering them 'something': a
language lab on the second floor; records and books where
you find the great trends that move our society; music for
research; works that explain an epoch. Products accompanied
by 'gray matter', this is the drugstore, but in a new style, with
something more, perhaps a bit of intelligence and human
warmth.

A drugstore can become a whole city: such as Parly 2, with its giant
shopping center, where 'art and leisure mingle with everyday life'; where each

residential group encircles a pool club (the center of attraction), a circular church, tennis courts ('the least of things'), elegant boutiques, and a library. Even the smallest ski resort is organized on the 'universalist' model of the drugstore, one where all activities are summarized, systematically combined and centered around the fundamental concept of 'ambiance.' Thus Idleness-on-the-Wasteful simultaneously offers you a complete, polymorphic and combinatorial existence:

> Our Mt Blanc, our Norway spruce forest; our Olympic runs,
> our 'park' for children; our architecture, carved, trimmed, and
> polished like a work of art; the purity of the air we breathe;
> the refined ambiance of our Forum, modeled after
> Mediterranean cities where, upon return from the ski slopes,
> life flourishes. Cafes, restaurants, boutiques, skating rinks,
> night clubs, cinemas, and centers of culture and amusement
> are all located in the Forum to offer you a life off the slopes
> that is particularly rich and varied. There is our closed circuit
> TV; and our future on a human scale (soon, we will be
> classified as a work of art by the department of cultural
> affairs).

We have reached the point where 'consumption' has grasped the whole of life; where all activities are sequenced in the same combinatorial mode; where the schedule of gratification is outlined in advance, one hour at a time; and where the 'environment' is complete, completely climatized, furnished, and culturalized. In the phenomenology of consumption, the general climatization of life, of goods, objects, services, behaviors, and social relations represents the perfected, 'consummated,' stage of evolution which, through articulated networks of objects, ascends from pure and simple abundance to a complete conditioning of action and time, and finally to the systematic organization of ambiance, which is characteristic of the drugstores, the shopping malls, or the modern airports in our futuristic cities.

Parly 2

'The largest shopping center in Europe.'

'Printemps, BHV, Dior, Prisunic, Lanvin, Frank et Fils,
Hediard, two cinemas, a drugstore, a supermarket, Suma, a
hundred other shops, all gathered in a single location!'

In the choice of shops, from groceries to high fashion, there are two requirements: progressive marketing and a sense of aesthetics.

The famous slogan 'ugliness doesn't sell' is outmoded, and could be replaced by 'the beauty of the surroundings is the precondition for a happy life': a two-story structure . . . organized around a central mall, with a main street and promenades on two levels; the reconciliation of the small and large shop and of the modern pace with the idleness of antiquity.

The mall offers the previously unexperienced luxury of strolling between stores which freely (*plain-pied*) offer their temptations without so much interference as glare from a display window. The central mall, a combination of rue de la Paix and the Champs Elysées, is adorned by fountains and artificial trees. Kiosks and benches are completely indifferent to seasonal changes and bad weather. An exceptional system of climate control, requiring eight miles of air conditioning ducts, creates a perpetual springtime.

Not only can anything be purchased, from shoestrings to an airline ticket, or located, such as insurance company, cinema, bank or medical service, bridge club and art exhibition, but one need not be the slave of time. The mall, like every city street, is accessible seven days a week, day or night.

Naturally, the shopping mall has instituted, for those who desire, the most modern form of payment: the 'credit card.' The card frees us from checks, cash, and even from financial difficulties at the end of the month. Henceforth, to pay you present your card and sign the bill. That's all there is to it. Each month you receive a bill which you can pay in full or in monthly instalments.

In the marriage between comfort, beauty, and efficiency, Parlysians discover the material conditions of happiness which the anarchy of older cities refuses them.

Here we are at the heart of consumption as the total organization of everyday life, as a complete homogenization. Everything is appropriated and simplified into the translucence of abstract 'happiness,' simply defined by the resolution of tensions. Expanded to the dimension of the shopping mall and the futuristic city, the drugstore is the *sublimation* of real life, of objective social life, where not only work and money are abolished, but the seasons disappear as well – the distant vestige of a cycle finally domesticated! Work, leisure, nature, and culture, all previously dispersed, separate, and more or less irreducible activities that produced anxiety and complexity in our real life, and in our 'anarchic and archaic' cities, have finally become mixed, massaged, climate controlled, and domesticated into the simple activity of perpetual shopping. All these activities have finally become desexed into a single hermaphroditic ambiance of style! Everything is finally *digested* and reduced to the same homogeneous fecal matter (this occurs, of course, precisely under the sign of the disappearance of *'liquid' currency*, the still too visible symbol of the *real* excretion (*fecalité*) of real life, and of the economic and social contradictions that previously haunted it). All that is past (passed): a *controlled*, lubricated, and *consumed* excretion (*fecalité*) is henceforth transferred into things, everywhere diffused in the indistinguishability of things and of social relations. Just like the Roman Pantheon, where the gods of all countries coexisted in a syncretism, in an immense 'digest,' the super shopping center, our new pantheon, our pandemonium, brings together all the gods, or demons, of consumption. That is to say, every activity, labor, conflict and all the seasons are abolished in the same abstraction. The substance of life, unified in this universal digest, can no longer have any *meaning*: that which produced the dream work, the poetic work, the work of meaning, that is to say the grand schemas of displacement and condensation, the great figures of metaphor and contradiction, which are founded on the lived articulation of distinct elements, is no longer possible. The eternal substitution of homogeneous elements alone remains. There is no longer a symbolic function, but an eternal combinatory of 'ambiance' in a perpetual Springtime.

Hypermarket and Hypercommodity[2]

From thirty kilometers all around, the arrows point you toward these large triage centers that are the hypermarkets, toward this hyperspace of the commodity where in many regards a whole new sociality is celebrated. It remains to be seen how the hypermarket centralizes and redistributes a whole region and population, how it concentrates and rationalizes time, trajectories, practices – creating an immense to-and-fro movement totally similar to that of suburban *commuters*, absorbed and ejected at fixed times by their work place.

At the deepest level, another kind of work is at issue here, the work of acculturation, of confrontation, of examination, of the social code, and of the verdict: people go there to find and to select objects-responses to all the questions they may ask themselves; or, rather, they *themselves* come *in response* to the functional and directed question that the objects constitute. The objects are no longer commodities: they are no longer even signs whose meaning and message one could decipher and appropriate for oneself, they are *tests*, they are the ones that interrogate us, and we are summoned to answer them, and the answer is included in the question. Thus all the messages in the media function in a similar fashion: neither information nor communication, but referendum, perpetual test, circular response, verification of the code.

No relief, no perspective, no vanishing point where the gaze might risk losing itself, but a total screen where, in their uninterrupted display, the billboards and the products themselves act as equivalent and successive signs. There are employees who are occupied solely in remaking the front of the stage, the surface display, where a previous deletion by a consumer might have left some kind of a hole. The self-service also adds to this absence of depth: the same homogeneous space, without mediation, brings together men and things – a space of direct manipulation. But who manipulates whom?

Even repression is integrated as a sign in this universe of simulation. Repression become deterrence is nothing but an extra sign in the universe of persuasion. The circuits of surveillance cameras are themselves part of the decor of simulacra. A perfect surveillance on all fronts would require a heavier and more sophisticated mechanism of control than that of the store itself. It would not be profitable. It is thus an allusion to repression, a 'signal' of this order, that is put in place; this sign can thus coexist with all the others, and even with the opposite imperative, for example those that huge billboards express by inviting you to relax and to choose in complete serenity. These billboards, in fact, observe and surveille you as well, or as badly, as the 'policing' television. The latter looks at you, you look at yourself in it, mixed with the others, it is the mirror without silvering (*tain*) in the activity of consumption, a game of splitting in two and doubling that closes this world on itself.

The hypermarket cannot be separated from the highways that surround and feed it, from the parking lots blanketed in automobiles, from the computer terminal – further still, in concentric circles – from the whole town as a total functional screen of activities. The hypermarket resembles a giant montage factory, because, instead of being linked to the chain of work by a continuous rational constraint, the agents (or the patients), mobile and decentered, give the impression of passing through aleatory circuits from one point of the chain to another. Schedules, selection, buying are aleatory as well, in contrast to work practices. But it is still a question of a chain, of a programmatic discipline, whose taboos are effaced beneath a veneer of tolerance, facility, and hyperreality. The hypermarket is already, beyond the factory and traditional institutions of capital, the model of all future forms of controlled socialization: retotalization in a homogeneous space-time of all the dispersed functions of the body, and of social life (work, leisure, food, hygiene, transportation, media, culture); retranscription of the contradictory fluxes in terms of integrated circuits; space-time of a whole operational simulation of social life, of a whole structure of living and traffic.

A model of directed anticipation, the hypermarket (especially in the United States) preexists the metropolitan area; it is what gives rise to metro areas, whereas the traditional market was in the heart of a city, a place where the city and the country came to rub elbows. The hypermarket is the expression of a whole lifestyle in which not only the country but the town as well have disappeared to make room for 'the metro area' – a completely delimited functional urban zoning, of which the hypermarket is the equivalent, the micromodel, on the level of consumption. But the role of the hypermarket goes far beyond 'consumption,' and the objects no longer have a specific reality there: what is primary is their serial, circular, spectacular arrangement – the future model of social relations.

The 'form' hypermarket can thus help us understand what is the end of modernity. The large cities have witnessed the birth, in about a century (1850–1950), of a generation of large, 'modern' stores (many carried this name in one way or another), but this fundamental modernization, linked to that of trans-portation, did not overthrow the urban structure. The cities remained cities, whereas the new cities are *satellized* by the hypermarket or the *shopping center*, serviced by a programmed traffic network, and cease being cities to become metro-politan areas. A new morphogenesis has appeared, which comes from the cybernetic kind (that is to say, reproducing at the level of the territory, of the home, of transit, the scenarios of molecular control that are those of the genetic code), and whose form is nuclear and satellitic. The hypermarket as *nucleus*. The city, even a modern one, no longer absorbs it. It is the hypermarket that estab-lishes an orbit along which suburbanization moves. It functions as an *implant* for the new aggregates, as the university or even the factory sometimes also does – no longer the nineteenth-century factory nor the decentralized factory that, without breaking the orbit of the city, is installed in the suburbs, but the montage factory, automated by electronic controls, that is to say corresponding to a totally deter-ritorialized function and mode of work. With this factory, as with the hypermarket or the new university, one is no longer dealing with functions (commerce, work, knowledge, leisure) that are autonomized and displaced (which still characterizes the 'modern' unfolding of the city), but with *a model of the disintegration of func-tions*, of the indeterminacy of functions, and of the disintegration of the city itself, which is transplanted outside the city and treated as a hyperreal model, as the nucleus of a metropolitan area based on synthesis that no longer has anything to do with a city. Negative satellites of the city that translate the end of the city, even of the modern city, as a determined, qualitative space, as an original synthesis of a society.

One could believe that this implantation corresponds to the rationalization of diverse functions. But, in fact, from the moment a function becomes hyperspecialized to the point of being capable of being projected from every element on the terrain 'keys in hand,' it loses the finality proper to it and becomes something else altogether: a polyfunctional nucleus, an ensemble of 'black boxes' with multiple input-outputs, the locus of convection and of destructuration. These factories and these universities are no longer factories or universities, and the hypermarkets no longer have the quality of a market. Strange new objects of which the nuclear power station is without a doubt the absolute model and from which radiates a kind of neutralization of the territory, a power of deterrence that, behind the apparent function of these objects, without a doubt constitutes their fundamental function: the hyperreality of functional nuclei that are no longer at all functional. These new objects are the poles of simulation around which is elaborated, in contrast to old train stations, factories, or traditional transportation networks, something other than a 'modernity': a hyperreality, a simultaneity of all the functions, without a past, without a future, an operationality on every level. And doubtless also crises, or even new catastrophes: May 1968 begins at Nanterre, and not at the Sorbonne, that is to say in a place where, for the first time in France, the hyperfunctionalization *extra muros* of a place of learning is equivalent to deterritorialization, to disaffection, to the loss of the function and of the finality of knowledge in a programmed neofunctional whole. There, a new, original violence was born in response to the orbital satellization of a model (knowledge, culture) whose referential is lost.

Absolute Advertising, Ground-Zero Advertising[3]

Today what we are experiencing is the absorption of all virtual modes of expression into that of advertising. All original cultural forms, all determined languages are absorbed in advertising because it has no depth, it is instantaneous and instantaneously forgotten. Triumph of superficial form, of the smallest common denominator of all signification, degree zero of meaning, triumph of entropy over all possible tropes. The lowest form of energy of the sign. This unarticulated, instantaneous form, without a past, without a future, without the possibility of metamorphosis, has power over all the others. All current forms of activity tend toward advertising and most exhaust themselves therein. Not necessarily advertising itself, the kind that is produced as such – but the *form* of advertising, that of a simplified operational mode, vaguely seductive, vaguely consensual (all the modalities are confused therein, but in an attenuated, agitated mode). More generally, the form of advertising is one in which all particular contents are annulled at the very moment when they can be transcribed into each other, whereas what is inherent to 'weighty' enunciations, to articulated forms of meaning (or of style) is that they cannot be translated into each other, any more than the rules of a game can be.

This long movement toward translatability and thus toward a complete combinatorial, which is that of *the superficial transparency of everything*, of their absolute *advertising* (of which professional advertising is, once again, only an episodic form), can be read in the vicissitudes of propaganda.

The whole scope of advertising propaganda comes from the October Revolution and the market crash of 1929. Both languages of the masses, issuing from the mass production of ideas, or commodities, their registers, separate at first, progressively converge. Propaganda becomes the marketing and merchandising of idea-forces, of political men and parties with their 'trademark image.' Propaganda approaches advertising as it would the vehicular model of the only great and veritable idea-force of this competing society: the commodity and the mark. This convergence defines a society – ours – in which there is no longer any difference between the economic and the political, because the same language reigns in both, from one end to the other; a society therefore where the political economy, literally speaking, is finally fully realized. That is to say dissolved as a specific power (as a historical mode of social contradiction), resolute, absorbed in a language without contradictions, like a dream, because traversed by purely superficial intensities.

A subsequent stage is crossed once the very language of the social, after that of the political, becomes confused with this fascinating solicitation of an agitated language, once the social turns itself into advertising, turns itself over to the popular vote by trying to impose its trademark image. From the historical destiny that it was, the social itself fell to the level of a 'collective enterprise' securing its publicity on every level. See what surplus value of the social each advertisement tries to produce: *werben werben* (advertise advertise) – the solicitation of the social everywhere, present on walls, in the hot and bloodless voices of female radio announcers, in the accents of the sound track and in the multiple tonalities of the image track that is played everywhere before our eyes. A sociality everywhere present, an absolute sociality finally realized in absolute advertising – that is to say, also totally dissolved, a vestige of sociality hallucinated on all the walls in the simplified form of a demand of the social that is immediately met by the echo of advertising. The social as a script, whose bewildered audience we are.

Thus the form of advertising has imposed itself and developed at the expense of all the other languages as an increasingly neutral, equivalent rhetoric, without affects, as an 'asyntactic nebula,' Yves Stourdzé would say, which envelops us from every side (and which at the same time eliminates the hotly controversial problem of 'belief' and efficacy: it does not offer signifieds in which to invest, it offers a simplified equivalence of all the formerly distinctive signs, and deters them with this very equivalence). This defines the limits of advertising's current power and the conditions of its disappearance, since today advertising is no longer a stake, it has both 'entered into our customs' and at the same time escaped the social and moral dramaturgy that it still represented twenty years ago.

It is not that people no longer believe in it or that they have accepted it as routine. It is that if its fascination once lay in its power to simplify all languages, today this power is stolen from it by another type of language that is even more simplified and thus more functional: the languages of computer science. The sequence model, the sound track, and the image track that advertising, along with the other big media, offers us – the model of the combinatory, equal distribution of all discourses that it proposes – this still rhetorical continuum of sounds, signs, signals, slogans that it erects as a total environment is largely overtaken, precisely in its function of simulation, by the magnetic tape, by the electronic continuum that is in the process of being silhouetted against the horizon of the end of this century. Microprocessing, digitality, cybernetic languages go much further in the direction of the absolute simplification of processes than advertising did on its humble – still imaginary and spectacular – level. And it is because these systems go further that today they polarize the fascination that formerly devolved on advertising. It is information, in the sense of data processing, that will put an end to, that is already putting an end to the reign of advertising. That is what inspires fear, and what is thrilling. The 'thrill' of advertising has been displaced onto computers and onto the miniaturization of everyday life by computer science.

The anticipatory illustration of this transformation was Philip K. Dick's papula – that transistorized advertising implant, a sort of broadcasting leech, an electronic parasite that attaches itself to the body and that is very hard to get rid of. But the papula is still an intermediary form: it is already a kind of incorporated prosthesis, but it still incessantly repeats advertising messages. A hybrid, then, but a prefiguration of the psychotropic and data-processing networks of the automatic piloting of individuals, next to which the 'conditioning' by advertising looks like a delightful change in fortune.

Currently, the most interesting aspect of advertising is its disappearance, its dilution as a specific form, or even as a medium. Advertising is no longer (was it ever?) a means of communication or of information. Or else it is over-taken by the madness specific to overdeveloped systems, that of voting for itself at each moment, and thus of parodying itself. If at a given moment, commodity was its own publicity (there was no other), today publicity has become its own commodity. It is confused with itself (and the eroticism with which it ridiculously cloaks itself is nothing but the autoerotic index of a system that does nothing but designate itself – whence the absurdity of seeing in it an 'alienation' of the female body).

As a medium become its own message (which makes it so that now there is a demand for advertising in and of itself, and that thus the question of 'believing' in it or not is no longer even posed), advertising is completely in unison with the social, whose historical necessity has found itself absorbed by the pure and simple *demand* for the social: a demand that the social function like a business, a group of services, a mode of living or of survival (the social must be saved just as nature must be preserved: the social is our niche) – whereas formerly it was a sort of revolution in its very project. This is certainly lost: the social has lost precisely this power of illusion, it has fallen into the register of supply and demand, just as work has passed from being a force antagonistic to capital to the simple status of employment, that is to say of goods (eventually rare) and services just like the others. One can thus create advertising for work, the joy of finding work, just as one will be able to create advertising for the social. And, today, true advertising lies therein: in the design of the social, in the exaltation of the social in all its forms, in the fierce, obstinate reminder of a social, the need for which makes itself rudely felt.

Folkloric dances in the metro, innumerable campaigns for security, the slogan 'Tomorrow I work' accompanied by a smile formerly reserved for leisure time, and the advertising sequence for the election to the Prud-hommes (an industrial tribunal): 'I don't let anyone choose for me' – an Ubuesque slogan, one that rang so spectacularly false, with a mocking liberty, that of proving the social while denying it. It is not by chance that advertising, after having, for a long time, carried an implicit ultimatum of an economic kind, fundamentally saying and repeating incessantly, 'I buy, I consume, I take pleasure,' today repeats in other forms, 'I vote, I participate, I am present, I am concerned' – mirror of a paradoxical mockery, mirror of the indifference of all *public* signification.

The opposite panic: one knows that the social can be dissolved in a panic reaction, an uncontrollable chain reaction. But it can also be dissolved in the opposite reaction, a chain reaction of *inertia*, each microuniverse saturated, autoregulated, computerized, isolated in automatic pilot. Advertising is the prefiguration of this: the first manifestation of an uninterrupted thread of signs, like ticker tape – each isolated in its inertia. Disaffected, but saturated. Desensitized, but ready to crack. It is in such a universe that what Virilio calls the aesthetic of disappearance gathers strength, that the following begin to appear: fractal objects, fractal forms, fault zones that follow saturation, and thus a process of massive rejection, of the abreaction or stupor of a society purely transparent to itself.

Like the signs in advertising, one is geared down, one becomes transparent or uncountable, one becomes diaphanous or rhizomic to escape the point of inertia – one is placed in orbit, one is plugged in, one is satellized, one is archived – paths cross: there is the sound track, the image track, just as in life there is the work track, the leisure track, the transport track, etc., all enveloped in the advertising track. Everywhere there are three or four paths, and you are at the crossroads. Superficial saturation and fascination.

Because fascination remains. One need only look at Las Vegas, the absolute advertising city (of the 1950s, of the crazy years of advertising, which has retained the charm of that era, today retro in some sense, because advertising is secretly condemned by the programmatic logic that will give rise to very different cities). When one sees Las Vegas rise whole from the desert in the radiance of advertising at dusk, and return to the desert when dawn breaks, one sees that advertising is not what brightens or decorates the walls, it is what effaces the walls, effaces the streets, the facades, and all the architecture, effaces any support and any depth, and that it is this liquidation, this reabsorption of everything into the surface (whatever signs circulate there) that plunges us into this stupefied, hyperreal euphoria that we would not exchange for anything else, and that is the empty and inescapable form of seduction.

> Language allows itself to be dragged along by its double, and joins the best to the worst for a phantom of rationality whose formula is 'Everyone must believe in it.' Such is the message of what unites us.
>
> J. L. Bouttes, *Le destructeur d'intensités*
> (The Destroyer of Intensities)

Advertising, therefore, like information: destroyer of intensities. Accelerator of inertia. See how all the artifices of meaning and of nonmeaning are repeated in it with lassitude, like all the procedures, all the mechanisms of the language of communication (the function of contact: you understand me? Are you looking at me? It will speak! – the referential function, the poetic function even, the allusion, the irony, the game of words, the unconscious), how all of that is staged exactly like sex in pornography, that is to say without any faith, with the same tired obscenity. That is why, now, it is useless to analyze advertising as language, because something else is happening there: a doubling of language (and also of images), to which neither linguistics nor semiology corresponds, because the function on the veritable operation of meaning, without the slightest suspicion of this caricatural exorbitance of all the functions of language, this opening onto an immense field of the mockery of signs, 'consumed' as one says in their mockery, *for* their mockery and the collective spectacle of their game without stakes – just as porno is a hypertrophied fiction of sex consumed in its mockery, for its mockery, a collective spectacle of the inanity of sex in its baroque assumption (it was the baroque that invented this triumphal mockery of stucco, fixing the disappearance of the religious in the orgasm of statues).

Where is the golden age of the advertising project? The exaltation of an object by an image, the exaltation of buying and of consumption through the sumptuary spending of advertising? Whatever the subjugation of publicity to the management of capital (but this aspect of the question – that of the social and economic impact of publicity – always remains unresolved and fundamentally insoluble), it always had more than a subjugated function, it was a mirror held out to the universe of political economy and of the commodity, it was for a moment their glorious imaginary, that of a torn-up world, but an expanding one. But the universe of the commodity is no longer this one: it is a world both saturated and in involution. In one blow, it lost both its triumphal imaginary, and, from the mirror stage, it passed in some sense to the stage of mourning.

There is no longer a staging of the commodity: there is only its obscene and empty form. And advertising is the illustration of this saturated and empty form.

That is why advertising no longer has a territory. Its recoverable forms no longer have any meaning. The Forum des Halles, for example, is a gigantic advertising unit – an operation of publicitude. It is not the advertising of a particular person, of any firm, the Forum also does not have the status of a veritable mall or architectural whole, any more than Beaubourg is, in the end, a cultural center: these strange objects, these supergadgets simply demonstrate that our social monumentality has become advertising. And it is something like the Forum that best illustrates what advertising has become, what the *public domain* has become.

The commodity is buried, like information is in archives, like archives are in bunkers, like missiles are in atomic silos.

Gone the happy and displayed commodity, now that it flees the sun, and suddenly it is like a man who has lost his shadow. Thus the Forum des Halles closely resembles a funeral home – the funereal luxury of a commodity buried, transparent, in a black sun. Sarcophagus of the commodity.

Everything there is sepulchral – white, black, salmon marble. A bunker-case – in deep, snobbish, dull black – mineral underground space. Total absence of fluids; there is no longer even a liquid gadget like the veil of water at Parly 2, which at least fooled the eye – here not even an amusing subterfuge, only pretentious mourning is staged. (The only amusing idea in the whole thing is precisely the human and his shadow who walk in *trompe l'oeil* on the vertical dais of concrete: a gigantic, beautiful gray, open-air canvas, serving as a frame to the *trompe l'oeil*, this wall lives without having wished to, in contrast to the family vault of *haute couture* and *prêt-à-porter* that constitutes the Forum. This shadow is beautiful because it is an allusion in contrast to the inferior world that has lost its shadow.)

All that one could hope for, once this sacred space was opened to the public, and for fear that pollution, as in the Lascaux caves, cause it to deteriorate irremediably (think of the waves of people from the RER), was that it be immediately closed off to circulation and covered with a definitive shroud in order to keep this testimony to a civilization that has arrived, after having passed the stage of the *apogee*, at the stage of the *hypogee*, of the commodity, intact. There is a fresco here that traces the long route traversed, starting with the man of Tautavel passing through Marx and Einstein to arrive at Dorothée Bis . . . Why not save this fresco from decomposition? Later the speleologists will rediscover it, at the same time that they discover a culture that chose to bury itself in order to definitively escape its own shadow, to bury its seductions and its artifices as if it were already consecrating them to another world.

M a s s   (S o c i o l o g y   o f) [4]

Mass languages

The languages of propaganda and advertising are mass languages, constituting the medium of a widespread socialization of messages which appear simultaneously with the advent, at the turn of the nineteenth century, of a practice of mass politics (through the course of the French Revolution and universal suffrage) and of mass production (through the course of the Industrial Revolution). Yet neither one nor the other – propaganda nor advertising – comes, respectively, fully into its own until after the October Revolution and the global crisis of 1929. And, at the same time, their respective fields (and their language) are brought so close that they merge. It is clear that advertising arises as a factor of the rescuscitation and consolidation of neo-capitalism, and is thus directly like a political practice. As for propaganda, it can be defined from the beginning as a true *marketing* and *merchandising* of the key ideas of men of politics and parties, with their 'brand images'.

More and more, propaganda and advertising converge today in a global strategy of human relations, in a style of communications and language. And it is in this contemporary convergence that they define a type of society such as our own in which there is no longer a difference between the economic and the political, because the same language dominates throughout them; a society, then, where 'political economy', literally speaking, is at last fully realized. There have always been techniques of commercial distribution or of political persuasion, but advertising and propaganda do not truly appear until a period when language aims at a total public and becomes by the same token totalitarian. This is the era of the media.

A structure of modernity

In a first phase, having been based upon a psychology of conditioned reflex, of anxiety and electroshock, that is to say, upon a mechanistic and metallurgical technique of human relations, this mass language is today oriented towards a psychology of contact, dialogue and feedback; in other words it is based upon a cybernetic technique of information understood as a system of integral relations. But, in any case, it is defined by a decisive rupture between a category of senders and a mass of receivers (citizens or consumers), a rupture which is distinct from the circuit of the right to speak amongst the members of a traditional group. With this type of mediatic language thus appears a characteristic structure of modernity: the technical and social division of communication and messages, which go to sanction and intensify the technical and social division involved in the production of material goods. With advertising and propaganda, linked to the emergence of the media and of the modern forms (press, cinema, radio, television), a collective regulation of unidirectional signs is erected with no possibility of any real response possible. (Who responds to the messages of advertising and propaganda?) It is in this sense that their language is 'totalitarian'. This unilateral regulation joins together with that of the production and distribution of material goods: a real political economy of the sign.

An operational language

In the functional order, what characterizes this type of language is the predominance of what Jakobson calls the 'conative function': the targeting of the receiver. These are 'operational' languages that aim to redirect the behaviour of the receiver. Of course, they also have a referential function: the one refers to consumer goods, the other to the management of the public entity. They pretend to instruct, explain, to speak the truth – they will always retreat, but seldom decisively and in one stroke, behind this value of information and objectivity. But the objective reference of this discourse, of which it speaks, largely disappears behind the mode in which it speaks: the imperative mode, the seductive mode. It is necessary to win support, to force consensus and, maximally – which is increasingly apparent with the current intensification of the media – the content is no more than an excuse for this function of seduction. The German term that designates the ensemble of these practices says it quite well: *werben* originally signified erotic and amorous solicitation. Commercial or political manipulation aiming to traffic in the dissemination of such a product or ideology is, without doubt, the manifest discourse of advertising and propaganda. On this level, then, their efficacy is completely relative: propaganda convinces bit by bit, its contents nullify, in a sense, one another. Advertising, we begin to see, does not sell (this is the least of its failings), but this does not matter: its strategy lies elsewhere. It is the generalized social integration of the *mise en scène* of all human relations according to the code they impose, of social control generalized through the injunctive or seductive mode, of abstraction and of spectacle (behind the ideology of contact, dialogue and solicitude). It is this form, that is to say, not at all such and such content, but a definite – totalitarian – form of social relations, that such language imposes.

Beyond truth and falsehood

At this point, advertising and propaganda mark a decisive (possibly definitive) phase in the history of communication. Western rationality has always been based, as regards discourse, upon the criteria of truth and falsehood. Now, this neolanguage, which has become the socially dominant language (it occupies not only the traditional fields of commerce or politics, but all the spheres of culture and social communication), is beyond or before truth and falsehood. It totally changes the traditional foundations of truth and falsehood, as it does not thrive on objective reality; rather, it thrives on codes and models. It does not thrive on reference or veracity; instead, it thrives on actual seduction, desire, ephemerality and, in the end, the code.

It is not at all that we are 'fooled': the objection that propaganda and advertising consist of lying, bluffing, and mystification is the weakest and most naive that we could raise. And so much so the complementary question, the veritable sea monster of the human sciences: do people believe it or not? Do advertisers and propagandists believe what they say? (They will be half-forgiven.) Do consumers and voters not believe what they are told? (They will be half-saved.) But the question does not lie there. One might be able to say, like DJ Boorstin in *The Image*, that the genius of Barnum, or of Hitler, was to discover not how easy it is to mislead the public, but how much the public loves to be fooled. Or further, that the most serious problems posed by advertising derive less from the unscrupulousness of those who fool us than from our pleasure in being fooled; they proceed less from the desire to seduce than from the desire to be seduced. Seductive hypothesis, but one that does not go deep enough: there is no manipulation of truth and falsehood at this level of language as it effaces, or radically displaces, the very conditions of truth or falsehood.

Advertising, for example, makes objects into events, but it constructs them as such on the basis of the elimination of their objective characteristics. It constructs them as spectacular current events, as myth, as model. The media do the same with 'historic' events: they construct them as models. They eventually construct them in all instances as models of simulation; propaganda does the same with ideas and concepts of social and political practice. 'Modern advertising comes into its own when an ad no longer functions as a spontaneous announcement, but becomes a new *fabrication*' (Boorstin). These models are not false: they have their logic and their coherence, but no longer derive them from ordinary reality – they come from their own code, becoming the reality principle. The deep seduction of these languages doubtless comes from this hypercoherence of a code, of a myth-ical and structural treatment where seduction can at last freely exercise itself, where desire can finally be fulfilled without the constraints of reality. (Simulation is also the foundation of all cybernetic and operational research, and one knows what social power of control this constitutes today.) Advertisers and propagandists are thus mythic operators, but not liars. This is more serious in a way because if they were merely liars, it would be easy to unmask them. Thus, all their art consists in the invention of persuasive displays that are neither true nor false.

In this way, their language refers entirely to a historical and social mutation which is accomplished under the logic of the sign. Mass communica-tion is beyond truth and falsehood in the way *that fashion is beyond beauty and ugliness, as political 'reason' is beyond good and evil*, and as objects are beyond utility and uselessness. All the great humanistic criteria of value, all those of a civilization of moral, aesthetic, practical judgement, fade away in our system of images and signs.

If this language of operational seduction is a mythic discourse, one could ask where the principle of its real efficacy lies. It is that of prophetic speech, of the *self-fulfilling prophecy*: 'the advertiser is master of a new art: the art of rendering things true in asserting that they are. It is an adept in the technique of prophecy who can accomplish this'. If, then, this language has its 'veracity', it is of a completely different type of verification that it concerns. Advertising does not suppose a prior reality, not even an object, but rather an ulterior confirmation, by virtue of the reality of a sign that it emits. It makes the object into a pseudo-event that will become the real event of daily life through the belief of the consumer in its discourse. The verification of its discourse is that part of consensus that it provokes, and its day of reckoning is the same as its unriddling: perfect definition of the magical sign, omnipotence of the artefact of the sign over the end of the world. Thus, the polls are where the most modern face of propaganda is legible: impossible to know if they reflect a public opinion or if the real vote is only the latest poll – but it is no longer a real event, it is nothing but the image of the model of anticipated simulation.

The internal logic of this neo-language

To this displacement of truth and falsehood and inversion of the referential and the code corresponds a completely different apparatus of the discourse from that of traditional logic.

Tautology

Logical articulation is replaced by tautology: 'Omo, there, that's washing'; 'The majority, that's you,' etc. This general schema culminates in the pure and simple incantation of the brand name or political slogan. All signs amount to one sign that equals itself: the brand or the slogan. It's on this recognizable sign, incessantly reduplicating itself, that this discourse comes to be indexed, contrary to open logical discourse. And it is this secret tautology, even if it wraps itself in significations and very rich rhetorical figures, that produces its efficacious causality and verisimilitude. It is this internal repetition that induces the 'magical' repetition of discourse in the event.

Paralogia of detail

Advertising is a total discourse of details, marginal differences, and partial truths reified in totality. It's the litany of the cigar lighter, the rhetoric of the accessory. In propaganda as well, technique consists in the orchestration of such detail, such selective aspects of reality, to the saturation of the ideological field. (Racist propaganda is exaltation derived from one, and only one, differential characteristic – race or blood – in order to make a total ideology.) There also, the logic of the whole and the part substitutes for that of truth and falsehood. The logic of displacement and substitution takes the place of dialectical articulation.

Paradox of the conjunction of incompatibles and the identity of contradictions

'At 140 km/h, you go faster in a Renault 16'. 'Three razors in one: when Phillips outdoes Phillips'. 'Living in the year 2000, today'. 'Invisibly dressed'.

This principle of magical synthesis, itself the corollary of tautology, is revealed in politics as the very language of terrorism and deterrence: it is the famous *Peace is war, war is peace*[5] of George Orwell's *Nineteen Eighty-Four* or, further, 'clean bomb', 'harmless fallout', and, once again, 'the majority, that's you'. Hypnotic language that no longer knows contradiction or negativity and thus returns to what Freud described as primary process: 'Thoughts which are mutually contradictory make no attempt to do away with each other, but persist side by side. They often combine to form condensations, *just as though there were no contradiction between them*, or arrive at compromises such as our conscious thoughts would never tolerate but such as are often admitted in our actions'.[6]

One sees this paradox again in the magical return of 'anti-advertising', which does nothing but mimic the critical distance *vis-à-vis* itself the better to pursue its objective – a bit like the artifice of the censor saying that 'one dreams within the dream'. It is by this same principle of total compatibility on the basis of the pure and simple manipulation of signs that the discourse can short-circuit and annex every other kind of discourse: scientific (biology of enzymes, technology, history), poetic and cultural, revolutionary discourse, discourse of the unconscious, objective discourse, critical discourse – all can be reintegrated as simulacra and serve as an alibi function for the mythic discourse.

Abolition of syntax

This is possibly the most characteristic tendency. 'Persil washes whiter' is not a sentence that is properly spoken, an articulate utterance. It is a frozen syntagm, identification, a solitary, full sign, a sentenceless indicative that declares itself an imperative. The same thing for 'change in continuity' or 'great party of the workers'. On the level of these language blocs, all discursivity is lost. Full signs, closed, indissociable, replaceable one by another within the indefinite paradigm that abolishes all syntax, whose actual function is to abolish syntax as a shifting dimension where meaning is made and unmade. Moreover, there is a proliferation in the neolanguage of prefixes, suffixes, superlatives (anti-, neo-, super-, etc.), generators of reflexive significations, of a desymbolized punchcard language.

The monopoly of speech

All these modalities place this discourse beyond reach of the game of logical reason, dialectic of sense and contradiction. It is in this way that it is terroristic, for it is here, through this manipulation of language on the level of the code, that it forbids all reciprocity of communication and any response to its messages (other than those already coded with its own signs). Certainly, advertising and propaganda *also* transmit ideological contents: dominant moral values, political dogmas – but once again, this 'manifest' ideology collides with individual or very complex collective systems of defence that are more solid than one thinks. It is true that everyone 'believes it', and that no one basically disbelieves. On the other hand, that's where this language is particularly efficacious; that's where everyone is vulnerable because it is a matter of the very structure of exchange: in its form, in this destructuration of traditional logic, in the imposition of this fixity of a social relation (always the same ones speak) and of this opaque circularity of signs (always the same signs sign). Nebulousness of closed signs, which can only be unilaterally deciphered, which are not any longer exchangeable between persons as in genuine symbolic discourse, and which really do not exchange either the role of sender or receiver. One sees that the neo-language, behind its ideology of dialogue and mass communication, prolongs and sanctions the dominant social

abstraction, and contributes to the broader reproduction of a society of monopolized speech and meaning, reinforcing by its very articulation *the power of the
ones and the irresponsibility of the others*.

Notes

1.   Extracts reprinted by permission of Sage Publishing Ltd from J. Baudrillard,
The Consumer Society, London: Sage, 1998.

2.   Extracts reprinted by permission of University of Michigan Press from
J. Baudrillard, *Simulacra and Simulation*, Ann Arbor: University of Michigan Press, 1994.
Translated by Sheila Faria Glazer.

3.   Ibid.

4.   Essay reprinted by permission of Sage Publishing Ltd from G. Genosko, *The
Uncollected Baudrillard*, London: Sage, 2001. Translated by Ben Freedman. Originally
published as 'Masse (Sociologie de)', in *Encyclopedia Universalis France*, Vol. 17 (1975),
pp 394–7. Reprinted in *Encyclopedia Universalis France*, Vol 14 (1990), pp 680–3.

5.   *Trans. note.* English in the original.

6.   *Trans. note.* Sigmund Freud, *The Interpretation of Dreams*, James Strachey
(trans.), PFL Vol 4, Harmondsworth: Penguin, 1986, p 755.

Chapter Six

THE IDEOLOGY OF TECHNIQUE

Technique as Social Practice[1]

All technical practice is social practice, all technicist practice is immersed in social determination. But such practice does not present itself in this way, claiming instead to be autonomous, innocent, claiming to be Technical Reason, grounded in Science. Such rationality underpins the ideology of Growth, which imposes itself on our society as if it were a moral code, and is where technicist practice, cut off from the social Reason for which it exists, becomes a technique *of the social* – or, more precisely, a technique of social manipulation, and therefore a technique of Power. The practical efficiency of Technique is transformed into social effectiveness. But this is too general a statement.[2]

It would be interesting to see how, in every era, the technical possibilities are taken into the logic of privilege. In the fifteenth and sixteenth centuries, those at the top of society kept the most advanced techniques to themselves, and used them for their celebrations. Over time, but most noticeably in the twentieth century, the most advanced techniques become those of the military, and the military is strictly in the hands of Power. The ruling classes generally only let filter down what is absolutely necessary for the reproduction of the productive forces. They even go so far as to wilfully organize stagnation or technical shortcomings.

Technique, and the uses made of it, has forever separated the social into distinct areas, categories, and zones of privilege. Discrimination through technique is a given throughout history.

However, it is only when technique emerges completely from religious, ritual, ludic, and corporative constraints, and when, along with the Industrial Revolution, it becomes a free productive force, that it elevates itself into the totalitarian myth of modern societies. This is still too simple, as it is not the effect on society as a whole of something overarching called 'technique' that we need to analyse. What we need to look at is how a society becomes stratified as a result of technique; what links the various classes or groups have with each other through technique as practice and as myth; what social strategy comes into being from that, and what sort of relation exists between social discrimination in the context of a value system called Technique, and social discrimination as it occurs in other value systems, such as Culture.

The myth would have it that whereas Culture is the site of hereditary inequality, *Technique would constitute a 'democratic' dimension*. According to this myth, individuals from any social background would be more naturally and spontaneously equal when it comes to Technique than they are with regard to Culture and Art (and there is even an inverse privilege attached to the under-privileged classes, being closer, as it is said, to the empirical world and the mechanical arts). According to this myth, *Technique would be a field that is more rational and, as a result, more democratic, as virtually anyone can get into it*, through a process of training and practice, as opposed to the subtler paths into Culture and Political Science. According to this myth, Technique would be an entirely innocent field, separate from politics. It would be innocent as it is to do with the mastery of Nature, whilst Culture, Economics, and Politics would be more directly involved in the organization and mastery of the social.

Against this myth, Technique is only an instrument for the mastery of nature and the freeing up of productive forces right at the beginning, or at an initial level. It is, at the same time, an instrument for restructuring social relations and for the development of a social rationality. Once it has gone beyond a particular level in the mastery of natural forces (and for us, this threshold has long been crossed), Technique becomes first and foremost an instrument of mastery and of social control. And this occurs in two ways: *directly, as an adjunct of Politics, and indirectly, as a mechanism of acculturation.*

The political dimension: with all social imperatives being subordinated to those of growth, and therefore to the controlled use of technology, the mastery of the conditions of technological research and the singular control of the higher technological operations (particularly military research) creates, for Power, a radically new privilege, upon which base the whole game of politics is played out. All investments and economic movements depend for their existence on this monopoly. The way in which secret rituals and the tools of the Sacred were possessed was never, in any period, in any society, as exclusive as the secrecy and technological manipulation by the State in our modern societies. We would of course have to investigate sociologically the structures of this monopoly, defining techno-political decision-making groups as opposed to there being pure technicians, on the one hand, and traditional politicians, on the other. We would also define the particular technicist ideology of such groups, as opposed to the technicist myths for the use of all, and so on.

The cultural dimension: Technique, far from unifying society on the basis of a form of discrimination between levels that is as certain, if not as traditionally and hereditarily based, as that of any cultural initiation. This system, like the other, works through institutions dedicated to technique, and a system of Technical Education as inferior vocation. The former (e.g. Research Institutes, The Science Academy, the National Centre for Social Research [CNRS], secret space and atomic research centres) sanction, at the highest level, Technique as a model and as a universal value. At this level, Technique is sublimated into Research and Science. Technical Education, particularly in our Western societies (even if we might wonder whether praise of technical values in the East is not fundamentally linked to economic objectives), remains ambiguous in its double, and shameful, link to the teaching of Culture and to theoretical scientific teaching.

The marked inequalities that this mechanism establishes in the real involvement in technical knowledge tend to be hidden by the diffuse mythology surrounding Technique. This hierarchy – official or officious – is subject to a very powerful social code. Between theoretical and vulgar practice, between a noble technical knowledge and applied knowledge, or, still lower, between the application of simple technical operating instructions and do-it-yourself, between access to treatises on nuclear physics and reading contemporary science or an instruction book on domestic techniques, there is a whole sliding scale of status, one that is regressive. Each one of these indicators reveals a particular social state, and comes together with others to assign each group its appropriate rank.

We need to be clear about this: it is about status, and not about knowledge. It is not about concrete differences in knowledge, which, logically speaking, have nothing to do with social hierarchy between people. It is about social *distinction*, class distinction based on the *quality* of knowledge taken as an indicator of *value*, and therefore of a *genuinely cultural system*. It is about a code of social designation that no longer works through a literary or artistic *habitus*, but through a lower or higher degree of *initiation* into the technical order.

In the social logic of culture, technical order, as a system, comes into play, and this, with relation to the system based on humanist values, as a parallel *system of acculturation* replacing the former and filling in (with very similar mechanisms) where the traditional system of acculturation would break down.

Technique constitutes one of the most powerful themes in mass culture. Within the population there are substantial social groups, essentially untouched by the genuinely cultural versions of culture, that are only capable of being integrated through the dreams, impulses, and fragmentary bits of knowledge given out in the field of technique.

The widespread phenomenon of autodidacticism – the standard process of catching up engaged in by the middle classes as they emerge as such – feeds, to a large extent, on technique. All those who are left by the wayside by scientific or cultural training attain their salvation, one way or another, through Technique. It is not that they have a natural inclination towards it. Rather it is the logic of the overall cultural system which assigns them to this subculture, which lives off the prestige of science, in unconscious resignation.

On top of the direct power that it confers through its political efficiency, Technique brings a parallel, *ideological power* that it acquires from the fact that it functions as a pseudo-culture. It is a secondary culture, destined, for the main part, for the uncultured classes, but is still a systematized culture, with its apparatus, its points of legitimacy, its mechanisms of transmission, its models and its norms – it functions, in short, like a total cultural system that comes to reinforce the other, so as to confirm the hierarchy of powers within society.[3]

So, we will only be able to capture the ambiguity of Technique if we analyse the position accorded it in the framework of an overall value system: rendered sacred as the ultimate means of power in the arena of international economics, technique is still an ignominious educational and cultural value. We also need to analyse how is it that our societies fail to autonomize technical values as worthwhile in their own right, and come to transcend this failure (or rationalize it) in a universalist myth of Technique.[4]

But, basically, if our societies do fail to rationalize technique as social practice (and not just as technical practice), this failure is precisely not an innocent one, for to rationalize the practice of technique would be equivalent to giving up the mystery of technique as a basis for social practice.

In a hierarchical society, technique, like many other things, is not supposed to be there to function, *but to provide the mystery of function*. And this mystery, which lays upon every technical product, every point technique occurs in the social body, is a social mystery.

The organization, as myth, of technique

Technique presents itself first and foremost in social terms – once outside the abstract and rational mode of pure technology – as a double system, one of systematic opposition between two terms where each justifies the other, with these two terms being: a Metatechnique, and an everyday practice. One is a transcendent Technique, brought into being in fiction, and the other is technique rendered mundane, reified as part of consumption.

This distortion of technique is often talked about in terms of spin-offs. Everyday life, maintained in a state of technical infantilism (for strategic reasons), benefits nonetheless from the spin-offs of high-level technique. This presumes an acceptance of the argument that there is uneven development of the different

sectors within social life, and behind this is the hypothesis that there is a theoretical unity, a transparency within technique, the glorious spread of which is
curtailed only by social structures.

In reality there is no technique other than that developed by people in
given social contexts, and no meaning of technique apart from that which it
acquires within social logic. This social logic, however, establishes technique from
the outset as a bipolar ideological system. Far from it being a case of social organization coming along to separate a unitary technique from its true principle, it
is the social, and it alone, which installs technique, and installs it as something
divided up, discontinuous. It is the social which gives technique (in its status of
social signifier) this logical distance between two poles as its basis.

Sublime technique, banal technique. Fiction, everydayness. Between the
two, no great distance, nor any 'spin-offs'; rather, a logical distance and a contradictory mutual involvement. In this, Technique is homologous to Culture – both
follow the same social logic. Furthermore, there is no Highbrow Culture which
would have *Mass Culture* as its 'spin-off' (in terms of individual versus mass-
produced item). There is, from the very beginning, an entire cultural system based
on the logical distance between Highbrow and Mass Culture, with one defining
itself in terms of the other, with each implying and also excluding the other. This
to the benefit of Highbrow Culture, which is the guardian of the definitive models.

In the same way it can be seen that Higher Technique, *in its very progress*,
has as its base the principle of the dividing up, through technique, of everyday
life, and also the giving over of the latter to the stereotypes of consumption. So
it is not at all an accident of society if everyday life is in a state of chronic technical under-development. This is far from being a malfunction, as it is a function
that obeys the *logic* of the system, just as a certain amount of poverty and hard-
ship is a functional element of the 'welfare state'.[5]

It is in this tactical doubling that the imaginary comes into play. Higher
Technique, cut off as it is from daily technical practice and muddled up with
Science, can come to serve as the imaginary of the banal technique of consumption, just as Highbrow Culture basically serves as the imaginary, in terms of being
the standard, for Mass Culture. The worship of technique that comes from nuclear

and space research, from futurism – all of this creation of new worlds, all this science fiction – can come into play through domestic gadgets, which, as a result, are not experienced as spin-offs, but are transfigured as signs and promise of a total Technical Revolution, the model for which is already there. This is hinted at throughout the wild and euphoric discourse on Technique (and this discourse always comes complete with a pessimistic moral discourse, which only serves to heighten the sense of intoxication). The average individual thinks themself a total citizen of the Technical Revolution, through the panel of their washing machine, but this panel, with its caricatural power, coming from an archaic world of functions, is in fact not doing anything at all except consigning them to the absence of any complete innovative, or restructuring technique, and this in turn is consumed as absence. In this way, the most insignificant of everyday objects implies the total functionality of a completed world of technique, beyond any social contradictions, beyond history. This is the other element of the social mystery mentioned earlier.

Technique, then, comes about in major, mythical, oppositions, such as that between rocket and car. In practice, the opposition between a technique seen as prestigious and one that is obsolete is no more than apparent. A whole civilization is clogged up in the concrete dictatorship of the car, and the fascination with the adventures of the space programme. These are the two poles of a systemic contradiction within which both technique and everyday life surround and are alienated one from another.

As a result of this systemic doubling, where one term works as the imaginary of the other, technical objects do not come directly into everyday life as mediators of new social functions and structures, but rather are *already mediated by the Idea of Technique*, and by a metaphysics of rationality.

This signifies, in concrete terms, that new objects and techniques are not lived as practical and social innovations, but as a sort of intermittent novelty, acquiring their fascination from their complicity with the Myth, the Future, the imaginary, and not at all from any possibility they might have of changing the present. This is how they come to be received as OBJECTS, *that is fixed and idealized as avant-garde SIGNS, populating an unreal everydayness*. This is how they fall into CONSUMPTION. And this with the following paradox: the more technically new they are, the more they are seen as aesthetic and destined for consumption by the wealthy.

So this is how Technique, which is immersed in everyday life, comes to be realized as science fiction, feeding an aesthetic of fascination and simulation, giving over all its power to the prestige to be had in consumption. The same thing happens, more or less, to any technical object or set of procedures, as happened to the filmmaker, as Edgar Morin showed convincingly in *Le Cinéma ou l'homme imaginaire (Cinema and Imaginary Man):* the immense possibilities for information, communication, and social change opened up at the beginning, in terms of a scientific technique of the image, fell away almost totally, and seemingly irrevocably, into the imaginary – leading to Cinema as Spectacle, and the Cinema of consumption.

Conclusion: 'Technique Totally in the Service of Everyday Life?'

If one allows that Technique presents itself, at the outset, and within the social logic of class, as just such a system described above, and therefore as a system of mythical transfiguration of real contradictions (those of everyday life and of social structures), then what about the revolutionary slogan that is Lefebvre's *'Technique Totally in the Service of Everyday Life?'*[6] In practice, for technique to bring about a revolution in everyday life, there would have to already have been a revolution of the whole system so as to make Technique something other than it is.

The hope of revolution is based on the premise that there is a fundamental rationality to the technical order that only needs to be freed and articulated through social reality in order to overturn it. But it is not that simple. Such a rational level of technique certainly does exist – in the form of technology. But whether as private individuals or as social subjects, we do not have anything to do with technology. What we have is technique in the form of a system of values and ideology. So what hope is there if Technique is the product (of the most efficient type) of the very social order the failure and contradictions of which are masked by Technique's rapid progress, thus taking away the possibilities of their resolution? How can we hope to put Technique in the service of a social revolution?

Up to a point, to do so would be to make the same mistake that lies in the claim that 'the police would come to be totally in the service of the collectivity', when, by definition, the police is social, and serves private interests and Power. The same could be said of Culture.

In short, we should avoid thinking of the technical dereliction of society as an accident that happened on the way, and that all we need do is to put technique back on the track, free up its potential, and life would be changed. We need to see that it is our society, itself, at its deepest level of organization, that reinvents Technique at every passing moment – as a dimension not of knowledge, but of salvation; as a mythical system and power strategy, as opposed to a rational instrumentality and revolutionary social practice.

In any case, there is no possibility of any revolutionary 'irruption' of technique in concrete society. In order for technical innovation to bring about real structural changes, there has first to be installed a *technical culture* – and that through the slow and difficult substitution of traditional culture by another value system. This would occur through a *whole, radically different, educational system*, different not so much in its content, but in its training *techniques*. We need to finally get out from the *Technique of the Spectacle of Technique*, and the myth that surrounds it, so that we recognise it through the principle of its functioning (which is that of 'capability and rational usage'),[7] and transport this principle right to the root of social training, if we want to really get rid of all the magic trickery.

Ephemeral and Durable[8]

The ephemeral is without doubt the truth of the future habitat. Mobile, variable, and retractable structures fit into the formal *demands of architects and the social and economic demands of modernity*. But this is only true in an ideal dimension. One must not lose sight that:

1. Neither the ephemeral nor the durable is an absolute and exclusive value. Only their constant relation and the multiple play of oppositions between them found a logic of cultural significations. One can reorient their relationship and bend it according to social rhythms in this sense, everything really pushes us toward an accelerated mortality of objects and structures. Nevertheless, the two terms only have meaning relative one to the other.

More precisely: if clothes, objects, appliances, and the car comply more and more with the norms of the ephemeral (but there is a limit), nothing says that they are not all together against 'inhabiting' it – this constituting a specific function which could be brutally or ideally assimilated to other aspects of consumption and fashion. The symbolic design of these is allocation and expense; the symbolic design of inhabiting is that of foundation and investment. To reduce the two to the same ephemeral synchrony is without doubt to liquidate an entire field of very rich contrasts. Yet there is lived culture (just as logic of sense) only in the tension between these two poles.

2. It is true that today there is a colossal social deficit that represents the fragmentary or whole construction as hard and durable: it contradicts economic rationality and social exchanges, the irreversible tendency toward greater social mobility, and flexibility of infrastructures. However, the latent psychological, familial, and collective functions of the 'hard' and the solid need to be taken into account – these are very powerful functions of integration that include them in the social 'budget'.

3. Some day, the ephemeral will perhaps be the collective solution, but for the time being, it is the monopoly of a privileged few whose economic and cultural standing permits them to call into question the myth of the durable.

It is because bourgeois generations have been able to enjoy the permanent and secular setting of property that some among them can today give themselves the luxury of renouncing stone houses and exalting the ephemeral: this custom belongs to them. All the generations of lower classes, by contrast, whose past opportunities for gaining access to the cultural models and to durable property were non-existent – to what does one want them to aspire, except to live the bourgeois model, build castles for themselves and their children, a derisory dynasty in stone residences or suburban housing tracts? How can one 'promote' for these classes today that they not regard property as sacred and agree right away to the ideality of mobile structures? They are doomed to desire things that last, and this longing only expresses the cultural destiny of their class.

Reciprocally, the cult of the ephemeral implies ideologically the privilege of the avant-garde: according to the eternal logic of cultural distinction, a privileged few savour the instantaneousness and mobility of architectural structures at the moment where the others just barely rise to the quadrature of their walls. Only the privileged classes are entitled to this year's models. The others are entitled to them once they have already changed.

If, therefore, in the logic of forms, the 'ephemeral' represents the truth of modernity, perhaps even the future formula of a rational and harmonious society, it still acquires an entirely different meaning in the present cultural system: if, in its foundational logic, culture plays continually on two *distinct* terms (ephemeral and durable), neither of which can be autonomized, in the socio-cultural system of class, this relation splits into two *distinctive* poles, from which the one – the ephemeral – autonomizes itself as a superior cultural model, relegating the other to 'obsolescence'.

This is not at all to disqualify the formal research of architects; but there is bitter derision in the fact that this research into social rationality precisely ends up reinforcing the irrational logic and strategy of the cultural system of class.

The Irony of Technology [9]

At the peak of our technological performance, the irresistible impression remains that something eludes us – not because we seem to have lost it (the real?), but because we are no longer in a position to see it: that, in effect, it is not we who are winning out over the world, but the world which is winning out over us. It is no longer we who think the object, but the object which thinks us. Once we lived in the age of the lost object; now it is the object which is 'losing' us, bringing about our ruin.

We very much labour under the illusion that the aim of technology is to be an extension of man and his power; we labour under the subjective illusion of technology. But today, this operating principle is thwarted by its very extension, by the unbridled virtuality we see outrunning the laws of physics and metaphysics. It is the logic of the system which, carrying it beyond itself, is altering its determinations. At the same time as reaching a paroxystic stage, things have also reached a parodic one.

All our technologies might, therefore, be said to be the instrument of a world which we believe we rule, whereas in fact the world is using this machinery to impose itself, and we are merely the operators. An objective illusion, then, similar to the one that prevails in the media sphere. The naive illusion about the media is that the political authorities use them to manipulate or mystify the masses. The opposite hypothesis is more subtle. Through the media, it is the masses who definitively modify the exercise of power (or what sees itself as such). It is at the point where the political authorities think they are manipulating them that the masses impose their clandestine strategy of neutralization and destabilization. Even if the two hypotheses are simultaneously valid, this is still the end of media Reason, the end of political Reason. Everything which will be done or said in the media sphere is, from this point on, ironically undecidable. The same hypothesis holds for the object of science. Through the most refined procedures we deploy to pin it down, is it not the object which dupes us and mocks our objective pretensions to analyze it? Scientists themselves are not, it seems, far from admitting this.

Can one advance the hypothesis that beyond the objective and critical phase there is an ironic phase of science, an ironic phase of technology? A proposition which would deliver us from the Heideggerian vision of technology as the final phase of metaphysics, from the retrospective nostalgia for being and from all unhappy critique in terms of alienation and disenchantment. And would put in its place a conception of the gigantic objective irony of this whole process, which would not be far from radical snobbery, from the post-historical snobbery Kojève spoke of.

It seems, in fact, that though the illusion of the world has been lost, the irony of the world, for its part, has passed into things. It seems that technology has taken into itself all the illusion it has caused us to lose, and that what we have in return for the loss of illusion is the emergence of an objective irony of this world. Irony as universal form of disillusionment, but also as the universal form of the stratagem by which the world hides behind the radical illusion of technology, and by which the mystery (of the continuation of the Nothing) conceals itself beneath the universal banality of information. Heidegger: 'When we look into the ambiguous essence of technology, we behold the constellation, the stellar course of the mystery.'

The Japanese sense the presence of a divinity in every industrial object. For us, that sacred presence has been reduced to a tiny ironic glimmer, a nuance of play and distantiation. Though this is, none the less, a spiritual form, behind which lurks the evil genius of technology which sees to it itself that the mystery of the world is well-guarded. The Evil Spirit keeps watch beneath artefacts and, of all our artificial productions, one might say what Canetti says of animals: that behind each of them there is a hidden someone thumbing his nose at us.

Irony is the only spiritual form in the modern world, which has annihilated all others. It alone is the guardian of the mystery, but it is no longer ours to exercise. For it is no longer a function of the subject; it is an objective function, that of the artificial, object world which surrounds us, in which the absence and transparency of the subject is reflected. The critical function of the subject has given way to the ironic function of the object. Once they have passed through the medium or through the image, through the spectrum of the sign and the commodity, objects, by their very existence, perform an artificial and ironic function. No longer any need for a critical consciousness to hold up the mirror of its double to the world: our modern world swallowed its double when it lost its shadow, and the irony of that incorporated double shines out at every moment in every fragment of our signs, of our objects, of our models. No longer any need to confront objects with the absurdity of their functions, in a poetic unreality, as the Surrealists did: things move to shed an ironic light on themselves all on their own; they discard their meanings effortlessly. This is all part of their visible, all too visible sequencing, which of itself creates a parody effect.

The aura of our world is no longer sacred. We no longer have the sacred horizon of appearances, but that of the absolute commodity. Its essence is promotional. At the heart of our universe of signs there is an evil genius of advertising, a trickster who has absorbed the drollery of the commodity and its *mise en scène*. A scriptwriter of genius (capital itself?) has dragged the world into a phantasmagoria of which we are all the fascinated victims.

All metaphysics is swept away by this turnabout in which the subject is no longer the master of representation ('I'll be your mirror'), but the operator of the objective irony of the world. It is, henceforth, the object which refracts the subject and imposes upon it its presence and its random form, its discontinuity, its fragmentation, its stereophony and its artificial instantaneity. It is the power of the object which cuts a swathe through the very artifice we have imposed on it. There is something of revenge in this: the object becomes a strange attractor. Stripped of all illusion by technology, stripped of all connotation of meaning and value, exorbitated – i.e. taken out of the orbit of the subject – it is then that it becomes a pure object, superconductive of illusion and non-meaning.

We are faced, ultimately, with two irreconcilable hypotheses: that of the extermination of all the world's illusion by technology and the virtual, or that of an ironic destiny of all science and all knowledge in which the world – and the illusion of the world – would survive. The hypothesis of a 'transcendental' irony of technology being by definition unverifiable, we have to hold to these two irreconcilable and simultaneously 'true' perspectives. There is nothing which allows us to decide between them. As Wittgenstein says: 'The world is everything which is the case'.

The Beaubourg Effect: Implosion or Deterrence? [10]

The Beaubourg effect, the Beaubourg machine, the Beaubourg *thing* – how to give it a name? Enigma of this carcass of flux and signs, of networks and circuits – the final impulse to translate a structure that no longer has a name, the structure of social relations given over to superficial ventilation (animation, self-management, information, media) and to an irreversibly deep implosion.

Monument to the games of mass simulation, the Pompidou Centre functions as an incinerator absorbing all the cultural energy and devouring it – a bit like the black monolith in *2001*: insane convection of all the contents that came there to be materialized, to be absorbed, and to be annihilated.

All around, the neighbourhood is nothing but a protective zone – remodelling, disinfection, a snobbish and hygienic design – but above all in a figurative sense: it is a machine for making emptiness. It is a bit like the real danger nuclear power stations pose: not lack of security, pollution, explosion, but a system of maximum security that radiates around them, the protective zone of control and deterrence that extends, slowly but surely, over the territory – a technical, ecological, economic, geopolitical glacis. What does the nuclear matter? The station is a matrix in which an absolute model of security is elaborated, which will encompass the whole social field, and which is fundamentally a model of deterrence (it is the same one that controls us globally, under the sign of peaceful coexistence and of the simulation of atomic danger).

The same model, with the same proportions, is elaborated at the Centre: cultural fission, political deterrence.

This said, the circulation of fluids is unequal. Ventilation, cooling, electrical networks – the 'traditional' fluids circulate there very well. Already the circulation of the human flux is less assured (the archaic solution of escalators in plastic sleeves, one ought to be aspirated, propelled, or something, but with a mobility that would be up to this baroque theatricality of fluids that is the source of the originality of the carcass). As for the material of the works, of objects, of books and the so-called polyvalent interior space, these no longer circulate at all. It is the opposite of Roissy, where from a futurist centre of 'spatial' design radiating toward 'satellites,' etc., one ends up completely flat in front of . . . traditional aeroplanes. But the incoherence is the same. (What happened to money, this other fluid, what happened to its mode of circulation, of emulsion, of fallout at Beaubourg?)

Same contradiction even in the behaviour of the personnel, assigned to the 'polyvalent' space and without a private work space. On their feet and mobile, the people affect a cool demeanour, more supple, very contemporary, adapted to the 'structure' of a 'modern' space. Seated in their corner, which is precisely not one, they exhaust themselves secreting an artificial solitude, remaking their 'bubble.' Therein is also a great tactic of deterrence: one condemns them to using all their energy in this individual defence. Curiously, one thus finds the same contradiction that characterizes the Beaubourg thing: a mobile exterior, commuting, cool and modern – an interior shrivelled by the same old values.

This space of deterrence, articulated on the ideology of visibility, of transparency, of polyvalency, of consensus and contact, and sanctioned by the blackmail to security, is today, virtually, that of all social relations. All of social discourse is there, and on this level as well as on that of the treatment of culture, Beaubourg flagrantly contradicts its explicit objectives, a nice monument to our modernity. It is nice to think that the idea did not come to some revolutionary spirit, but to the logicians of the established order, deprived of all critical intelligence, and thus closer to the truth, capable, in their obstinacy, of putting in place a machine that is fundamentally uncontrollable, that in its very success escapes them, and that is the most exact reflection, even in its contradictions, of the current state of things.

Certainly, all the cultural contents of Beaubourg are anachronistic, because only an empty interior could correspond to this architectural envelope. The general impression being that everything here has come out of a coma, that everything wants to be animation and is only reanimation, and that this is good because culture is dead, a condition that Beaubourg admirably retraces, but in a dishonest fashion, whereas one should have triumphantly accepted this death and created a monument or an antimonument equivalent to the phallic inanity of the Eiffel Tower in its time. Monument to total disconnection, to hyperreality and to the implosion of culture – achieved today for us in the effect of transistorized circuits always threatened by a gigantic short circuit.

Beaubourg is already an imperial compression – figure of a culture already crushed by its own weight – like moving automobiles suddenly frozen in a geometric solid. Like the cars of Caesar, survivors of an ideal accident, no longer external, but internal to the metallic and mechanical structure, and which would have produced tons of cubic scrap iron, where the chaos of tubes, levers, frames, of metal and human flesh inside is tailored to the geometric size of the smallest possible space – thus the culture of Beaubourg is ground, twisted, cut up, and pressed into its smallest simple elements – a bundle of defunct transmissions and metabolisms, frozen like a science-fiction mecanoid.

But instead of breaking and compressing all culture here in this carcass that in any case has the appearance of a compression, instead of that, one *exhibits* Caesar there. One exhibits Dubuffet and the counterculture, whose inverse simulation acts as a referential for the defunct culture. In this carcass that could have served as a mausoleum to the useless operationality of signs, one reexhibits Tinguely's ephemeral and autodestructive machines under the sign of the eternity of culture. Thus one neutralizes everything together: Tinguely is embalmed in the museal institution, Beaubourg falls back on its supposed artistic contents.

Fortunately, this whole simulacrum of cultural values is annihilated in advance by the external architecture. Because this architecture, with its networks of tubes and the look it has of being an expo or world's fair building, with its (calculated?) fragility deterring any traditional mentality or monumentality, overtly proclaims that our time will never again be that of duration, that our only temporality is that of the accelerated cycle and of recycling, that of the circuit and of the transit of fluids. Our only culture in the end is that of hydrocarbons, that of refining, cracking, breaking cultural molecules and of their recombination into synthesized products. This, the Beaubourg Museum wishes to conceal, but the Beaubourg cadaver proclaims. And this is what underlies the beauty of the cadaver and the failure of the interior spaces. In any case, the very ideology of 'cultural production' is antithetical to all culture, as is that of visibility and of the polyvalent space: culture is a site of the secret, of seduction, of initiation, of a restrained and highly ritualized symbolic exchange. Nothing can be done about it. Too bad for the masses, too bad for Beaubourg.

What should, then, have been placed in Beaubourg?

Nothing. The void that would have signified the disappearance of any culture of meaning and aesthetic sentiment. But this is still too romantic and destructive, this void would still have had value as a masterpiece of anticulture.

Perhaps revolving strobe lights and gyroscopic lights, striating the space, for which the crowd would have provided the moving base element?

In fact, Beaubourg illustrates very well that an order of simulacra only establishes itself on the alibi of the previous order. Here, a cadaver all in flux and surface connections gives itself as content a traditional culture of depth. An order of prior simulacra (that of meaning) furnishes the empty substance of a subsequent order, which, itself, no longer even knows the distinction between signifier and signified, nor between form and content.

The question: 'What should have been placed in Beaubourg?' is thus absurd. It cannot be answered because the topical distinction between interior and exterior should no longer be posed. There lies our truth, the truth of Möbius – doubtless an unrealizable utopia, but which Beaubourg still points to as right, to the degree to which any of its contents is a *countermeaning* and annihilated in advance by the form.

Yet – yet . . . if you had to have something in Beaubourg – it should have been a labyrinth, a combinatory, infinite library, an aleatory redistribution of destinies through games or lotteries – in short, the universe of Borges – or even the circular Ruins: the slowed-down enchainment of individuals dreamed up by each other (not a dreamworld Disneyland, a laboratory of practical fiction). An experimentation with all the different processes of representation: defraction, implosion, slow motion, aleatory linkage and decoupling – a bit like at the Exploratorium in San Francisco or in the novels of Philip K. Dick – in short a culture of simulation and of fascination, and not always one of production and meaning: this is what might be proposed that would not be a miserable anticulture. Is it possible? Not here, evidently. But this culture takes place elsewhere, everywhere, nowhere. From today, the only real cultural practice, that of the masses, ours (there is no longer a difference), is a manipulative, aleatory practice, a labyrinthine practice of signs, and one that no longer has any meaning.

In another way, however, it is not true that there is no coherence between form and content at Beaubourg. It is true if one gives any credence to the official cultural project. But exactly the opposite occurs there. Beaubourg is nothing but a huge effort to transmute this famous traditional culture of meaning into the aleatory order of signs, into an order of simulacra (the third) that is completely homogeneous with the flux and pipes of the facade. And it is in order to prepare the masses for this new semiurgic order that one brings them together here – with the opposite pretext of acculturating them to meaning and depth.

One must thus start with this axiom: Beaubourg is a *monument of cultural deterrence*. Within a museal scenario that only serves to keep up the humanist fiction of culture, it is a veritable fashioning of the death of culture that takes place, and it is a veritable *cultural mourning* for which the masses are joyously gathered.

And they throw themselves at it. There lies the supreme irony of Beaubourg: the masses throw themselves at it not because they salivate for that culture which they have been denied for centuries, but because they have for the first time the opportunity to massively participate in this great mourning of a culture that, in the end, they have always detested.

The misunderstanding is therefore complete when one denounces Beaubourg as a cultural mystification of the masses. The masses, themselves, rush there to enjoy this execution, this dismemberment, this operational prostitution of a culture finally truly liquidated, including all counterculture that is nothing but its apotheosis. The masses rush toward Beaubourg as they rush toward disaster sites, with the same irresistible élan. Better: they *are* the disaster of Beaubourg. Their number, their stampede, their fascination, their itch to see everything is objectively a deadly and catastrophic behaviour for the whole undertaking. Not only does their weight put the building in danger, but their adhesion, their curiosity annihilates the very contents of this culture of animation. This rush can no longer be measured against what was proposed as the cultural objective, it is its radical negation, in both its excess and success. It is thus the masses who assume the role of catastrophic agent in this structure of catastrophe, *it is the masses themselves who put an end to mass culture*.

Circulating in the space of transparency, the masses are certainly converted into flux, but at the same time, through their opacity and inertia, they put an end to this 'polyvalent' space. One invites the masses to participate, to simulate, to play with the models – they go one better: they participate and manipulate so well that they efface all the meaning one wants to give to the operation and put the very infrastructure of the edifice in danger. Thus, always a sort of parody, a hypersimulation in response to cultural simulation, transforms the masses, who should only be the livestock of culture, into the agents of the execution of this culture, of which Beaubourg was only the shameful incarnation.

One must applaud this success of cultural deterrence. All the antiartists, leftists, and those who hold culture in contempt have never even got close to approaching the dissuasive efficacy of this monumental black hole that is Beaubourg. It is a truly revolutionary operation, precisely because it is involuntary, *insane* and uncontrolled, whereas any operation meant to put an end to culture only serves, as one knows, to resurrect it.

To tell the truth, the only content of Beaubourg is the masses themselves, whom the building treats like a converter, like a black box, or, in terms of input-output, just like a refinery handles petroleum products or a flood of unprocessed material.

It has never been so clear that the content – here, culture, elsewhere, information or commodities – is nothing but the phantom support for the operation of the medium itself, whose function is always to induce mass, to produce a homogeneous human and mental flux. An immense to-and-fro movement similar to that of suburban commuters, absorbed and ejected at fixed times by their workplace. And it is precisely work that is at issue here – a work of testing, polling, and directed interrogation: the people come here to select objects-responses to all the questions they might ask themselves, or rather *they come themselves in response to* the functional and directed question that the objects constitute. More than a chain of work it is thus a question of a programmatic discipline whose constraints have been effaced behind a veneer of tolerance. Well beyond traditional institutions of capital, the hypermarket, or the Beaubourg 'hypermarket of culture,' is already the model of all future forms of controlled socialization: retotalization in a homogeneous space-time of all the dispersed functions of the body and of social life (work, leisure, media culture), retranscription of all the contradictory currents in terms of integrated circuits. Space-time of a whole operational simulation of social life.

For that, the mass of consumers must be equivalent or homologous to the mass of products. It is the confrontation and the fusion of these two masses that occurs in the hypermarket as it does at Beaubourg, and that makes of them something very different from the traditional sites of culture (monuments, museums, galleries, libraries, community arts centres, etc.). Here a critical mass beyond which the commodity becomes hypercommodity, and culture hyperculture, is elaborated – that is to say no longer linked to distinct exchanges or determined needs, but to a kind of total descriptive universe, or integrated circuit that implosion traverses through and through – incessant circulation of choices, readings, references, marks, decoding. Here cultural objects, as elsewhere the objects of consumption, have no other end than to maintain you in a state of mass integration, of transistorized flux, of a magnetized molecule. It is what one comes to learn in a hypermarket: hyperreality of the commodity – it is what one comes to learn at Beaubourg: the hyperreality of culture.

Already with the traditional museum this cutting up, this regrouping, this interference of all cultures, this unconditional aestheticization that constitutes the hyperreality of culture begins, but the museum is still a memory. Never, as it did here, has culture lost its memory in the service of stockpiling and functional redistribution. And this translates a more general fact: that throughout the 'civilized' world the construction of stockpiles of objects has brought with it the complementary process of stockpiles of people – the line, waiting, traffic jams, concentration, the camp. That is 'mass production,' not in the sense of a massive production or for use by the masses, but the production of *the masses*. The masses as the final product of all sociality, and, at the same time, as putting an end to sociality, because these masses that one wants us to believe *are* the social, are on the contrary the site of the implosion of the social. *The masses are the increasingly dense sphere in which the whole social comes to be imploded, and to be devoured in an uninterrupted process of simulation.*

Whence this concave mirror: it is from seeing the masses in the interior that the masses will be tempted to rush in. Typical marketing method: the whole ideology of transparency here takes on its meaning. Or again: it is in staging a reduced ideal model that one hopes for an accelerated gravitation, an automatic agglutination of culture as an automatic agglomeration of the masses. Same process: nuclear operation of a chain reaction, or specular operation of white magic.

Thus for the first time, Beaubourg is at the level of culture what the hypermarket is at the level of the commodity: *the perfect circulatory operator*, the demonstration of anything (commodity, culture, crowd, compressed air) *through its own accelerated circulation.*

But if the supply of objects brings along with it the stockpiling of men, the latent violence in the supply of objects brings with it the inverse violence of men.

Every stock is violent and there is a specific violence in any mass of men also, because of the fact that it implodes – a violence proper to its gravitation, to its densification around its own locus of inertia. The masses are a locus of inertia and through that a locus of a completely new, inexplicable violence different from explosive violence.

Critical mass, implosive mass. Beyond thirty thousand it poses the risk of 'bending' the structure of Beaubourg. If the masses magnetized by the structure become a destructive variable of the structure itself – if those who conceived of the project wanted this (but how to hope for this?), if they thus programmed the chance of putting an end with one blow to both architecture and culture – then Beaubourg constitutes the most audacious object and the most successful happening of the century!

Make Beaubourg bend! New motto of a revolutionary order. Useless to set fire to it, useless to contest it. Do it! It is the best way of destroying it. The success of Beaubourg is no longer a mystery: the people go there *for that*, they throw themselves on this building, whose fragility already breathes catastrophe, with the single goal of making it bend.

Certainly they obey the imperative of deterrence: one gives them an object to consume, a culture to devour, an edifice to manipulate. But at the same time they expressly aim, and without knowing it, at this annihilation. The onslaught is the only act the masses can produce as such – a projectile mass that challenges the edifice of mass culture, that wittily replies with its *weight* (that is to say with the characteristic most deprived of meaning, the stupidest, the least cultural one they possess) to the challenge of culturality thrown at it by Beaubourg. To the challenge of mass acculturation to a sterilized culture, the masses respond with a destructive irruption, which is prolonged in a brutal manipulation. To mental deterrence the masses respond with a direct physical deterrence. It is their own challenge. Their ruse, which is to respond in the very terms by which they are solicited, but beyond that, to respond to the simulation in which one imprisons them with an enthusiastic social process that surpasses the objectives of the former and acts as a destructive hypersimulation.

People have the desire to take everything, to pillage everything, to swallow everything, to manipulate everything. Seeing, deciphering, learning does not touch them. The only massive affect is that of manipulation. The organizers (and the artists and intellectuals) are frightened by this uncontrollable watchfulness, because they never count on anything but the apprenticeship of the masses to the *spectacle* of culture. They never count on this active, destructive fascination, a brutal and original response to the gift of an incomprehensible culture, an attraction that has all the characteristics of breaking and entering and of the violation of a sanctuary.

Beaubourg could have or should have disappeared the day after the inauguration, dismantled and kidnapped by the crowd, which would have been the only possible response to the absurd challenge of the transparency and democracy of culture – each person taking away a fetishized bolt of this culture itself fetishized.

The people come to *touch*, they look as if they are touching, their gaze is only an aspect of tactile manipulation. It is certainly a question of a tactile universe, no longer a visual or discursive one, and the people are directly implicated in a process: to manipulate/to be manipulated, to ventilate/to be ventilated, to circulate/to make circulate, which is no longer of the order of representation, nor of distance, nor of reflection. It is something that is part of panic, and of a world in panic.

Panic in slow motion, no external variable. It is the violence internal to a saturated ensemble. *Implosion.*

Beaubourg cannot even burn, everything is foreseen. Fire, explosion, destruction are no longer the imaginary alternative to this type of building. It is implosion that is the form of abolishing the 'quaternary' world, both cybernetic and combinatory.

Subversion, violent destruction is what corresponds to a mode of production. To a universe of networks, of combinatory theory, and of flow correspond reversal and implosion.

The same for institutions, the state, power, etc. The dream of seeing all that explode by dint of contradictions is precisely nothing but a dream. What is produced in reality is that the institutions implode of themselves, by dint of ramifications, feedback, overdeveloped control circuits. *Power implodes*, this is its current mode of disappearance.

Such is the case for the city. Fires, war, plague, revolutions, criminal marginality, catastrophes: the whole problematic of the anticity, of the negativity internal or external to the city, has some archaic relation to its true mode of annihilation.

Even the scenario of the underground city – the Chinese version of the burial of structures – is naive. The city does not repeat itself any longer according to a schema of *reproduction* still dependent on the general schema of production, or according to a schema of resemblance still dependent on a schema of representation. (That is how one still restored after the Second World War). The city no longer revives, even deep down – it is remade starting from a sort of genetic code that makes it possible to repeat it indefinitely starting with an accumulated cybernetic memory. Gone even the Borgesian utopia, of the map coextensive with the territory and doubling it in its entirety: today the simulacrum no longer goes by way of the double and of duplication, but by way of genetic miniaturization. End of representation and implosion, there also, of the whole space in an infinitesimal memory, which forgets nothing, and which belongs to no one. Simulation of an immanent, increasingly dense, irreversible order, one that is potentially saturated and that will never again witness the liberating explosion.

We *were* a culture of liberating violence (rationality). Whether it be that of capital, of the liberation of productive forces, of the irreversible extension of the field of reason and of the field of value, of the conquered and colonized space including the universal – whether it be that of the revolution, which anticipates the future forms of the social and of the energy of the social – the schema is the same: that of an expanding sphere, whether through slow or violent phases, that of a liberated energy – the imaginary of radiation.

The violence that accompanies it is that of a wider world: it is that of production. This violence is dialectical, energetic, cathartic. It is the one we have learned to analyze and that is familiar to us: that which traces the paths of the social and which leads to the saturation of the whole field of the social. It is a violence that is *determined*, analytical, liberating.

A whole other violence appears today, which we no longer know how to analyze, because it escapes the traditional schema of explosive violence: *implosive* violence that no longer results from the extension of a system, but from its saturation and its retraction, as is the case for physical stellar systems. A violence that follows an inordinate densification of the social, the state of an overregulated system, a network (of knowledge, information, power) that is overencumbered, and of a hypertrophic control investing all the interstitial pathways.

This violence is unintelligible to us because our whole imaginary has as its axis the logic of expanding systems. It is indecipherable because undetermined. Perhaps it no longer even comes from the schema of indeterminacy. Because the aleatory models that have taken over from classical models of determination and causality are not fundamentally different. They translate the passage of defined systems of expansion to systems of production and expansion on all levels – in a star or in a rhizome, it doesn't matter – all the philosophies of the release of energy, of the irradiation of intensities and of the molecularization of desire go in the same direction, that of a saturation as far as the interstitial and the infinity of networks. The difference from the molar to the molecular is only a modulation, the last perhaps, in the fundamental energetic process of expanding systems.

Something else if we move from a millennial phase of the liberation and disconnection of energies to a phase of implosion, after a kind of maximum radiation (see Bataille's concepts of loss and expenditure in this sense, and the solar myth of an inexhaustible radiation, on which he founds his sumptuary anthropology: it is the last explosive and radiating myth of our philosophy, the last fire of artifice of a fundamentally general economy, but this no longer has any meaning for us), to a phase of the *reversion of the social* – gigantic reversion of a field once the point of saturation is reached. The stellar systems also do not cease to exist once their radiating energy is dissipated: they implode according to a process that is at first slow, and then progressively accelerates – they contract at a fabulous speed, and become involutive systems, which absorb all the surrounding energies, so that they become black holes where the world as we know it, as radiation and indefinite energy potential, is abolished.

Perhaps the great metropolises – certainly these if this hypothesis has any meaning – have become sites of implosion in this sense, sites of the absorption and reabsorption of the social itself whose golden age, contemporaneous with the double concept of capital and revolution, is doubtless past. The social involutes slowly or brutally, in a field of inertia, which already envelops the political. (The opposite energy?) One must stop oneself from taking implosion for a negative process – inert, regressive – like the one language imposes on us by exalting the opposite terms of evolution, of revolution. Implosion is a process specific to incalculable consequences. May 1968 was without a doubt the first implosive episode, that is to say contrary to its rewriting in terms of revolutionary prosopopeia, a first violent reaction to the saturation of the social, a retraction, a challenge to the hegemony of the social, in contradiction, moreover, to the ideology of the participants themselves, who thought they were going further into the social – such is the imaginary that still dominates us – and moreover a good part of the events of 1968 were still able to come from that revolutionary dynamic and explosive violence, but something else began at the same time there: the violent involution of the social, determined on that score, and the consecutive and sudden implosion of power, in a brief moment of time, but that never stopped afterward – fundamentally it is that which continues, the implosion, of the social, of institutions, of power – and not at all an unlocatable revolutionary dynamic. On the contrary, revolution itself, the idea of revolution also implodes, and this implosion carries weightier consequences than the revolution itself.

Certainly, since 1968, and thanks to 1968, the social, like the desert, grows – participation, management, generalized self-management, etc. – but at the same time it comes close in multiple places, more numerous than in 1968, to its disaffection and to its total reversion. Slow seism, intelligible to historical reason.

Notes

1. Essay reprinted by permission of Sage Publishers Ltd from G. Genosko, *The Uncollected Baudrillard*, London: Sage, 2001. Translated by Paul Hegarty. Originally published as 'La Pratique Sociale de la Technique', *Utopie* 2/3 (1969): pp 147–55.

2. *Trans. note.* The word 'technique' in French approaches the sense 'technology' now has in English. I have kept 'technique' as it implies process and procedure and, as will be clear later in the essay, is to be distinguished from technology. For this reason, 'technique' in the original should not be deemed to have been simply the contemporary word for technology.

3. The socialist countries have encouraged the high valuation of a technical culture. However, it seems that after a while (in Hungary and Yugoslavia), the hierarchy of traditional values, briefly overturned, tends to return, to the benefit of cultural values. In any case, profound changes in the cultural habitus can only come about in the long term.

4. *Trans. note.* Here, the original text directs the reader to the footnote that appeared at the end of the previous paragraph.

5. *Trans. note.* English in the original.

6. None of this excludes the *real* changes that technique brings about each day in everyday life or in social relations. These are undeniable, and considerable, only these changes work *inside a system* whose function is precisely that of controlling the evolution of the system, and making sure that the changes never establish any overt contradiction.

7. Strictly speaking, this principle has nothing to do with actually existing sciences or techniques. We need to remove 'Technique' from its use as an absolute category, to return it to its concrete efficiency, where it is always technique of something – of rational training and usage.

8. Essay reprinted by permission of Sage Publishers Ltd from G. Genosko, *The Uncollected Baudrillard*, London: Sage, 2001. Translated by Dylan Wood. Originally published as a marginal note in Jean Aubert's 'Devenir suranné', *Utopie* 1 (May 1967): pp 95–6.

9. Extract reprinted by permission of Verso from Jean Baudrillard, *The Perfect Crime*, London, 1996. Translated by Chris Turner.

10. Essay reprinted by permission of University of Michigan Press from Jean Baudrillard, Simulcra and Simulation, Ann Artbor. University of Michigan Press, 1994. Translated by Sheila Faria Glazer.

Chapter Seven

THE AESTHETIC SUICIDE

Questions of Strategy[1]
The fact is that I practise this taste for the absurd quite
religiously. *Alfred Hitchcock*

J BAUDRILLARD: Jean, you start from the idea that architecture cannot develop into autarky; that to make it exist, it must be considered in the mode of significations, and that puzzles me. From the moment that there exists a register (let's say a savage one) that needs no interpretation, does not giving signification open the way not to what one might call a semiurgy, but to linguistic and semiological re-writing . . . to absolute danger? On one hand there would be the current pathology of architecture which would be its hypostasis, on the other there would be objects, unidentified super-objects, gadgets . . . and to escape from them both, you would use paradoxical strategies; but these strategies are still yours, it is still you who determines what architecture should be. Myself, I'm not sure whether we should reject the brutal touchdown of these types of extra-terrestrial objects that can be terrifying or monstrous, like Beaubourg, or like all the current grand projects which collide with the city.

P GOULET: In an unforeseeable manner?

JB Yes, all the intentions behind the Beaubourg project have been denied by the object. Although based on positive perspectives (participation, communication etc.), in the end the project has been completely confounded by reality, by the hyperreality of the object. In the object, there is an inhumanity that contradicts all the project's human intentions. This reversal will have been in some way a sort of destiny for Beaubourg. And you can't possibly turn this towards more coherent and rational perspectives; it belongs to the object, to its inescapable fatality, from which perhaps we shouldn't wish to free it! On the contrary, shouldn't we exploit it, play it to the full to rediscover this paradox, this enigma, this radical surprise which can only come from the object? Pure objectality is the worst of things: it is a hell, but at the same time, it is probably a destiny[1]!

J NOUVEL: In *America*, you describe how in New York an anti-architecture that is ultimately positive has been built upon *a priori* atrocious and inhumane foundations. I believe in these architectural climates. They explain why a tower doesn't have the same signification in Paris as in New York. It's the friction, the density, the concentration of this city that make something happen there and that makes this something, naturally, bypass the architects.

JB: Koolhaas's book *Delirious New York* had a very nice idea: the vision of the Coney Island theme park as a project for Manhattan, seen thus as a super-production that had however become the apex of architecture or anti-architecture (but it's the same thing at that point). What I like about this idea is this invention (or re-invention) of the project long after the object exists, this laying bare of the 'precession' of the object over the project. This type of object, which is of course the opposite of the gadget object, comes from elsewhere, and always surprises you! I don't deny the need to take account of the spirit of the place, but the object must subsequently be able to escape from its creator and its users. We can rely on the users: I don't think there is a single example of architecture that they haven't hijacked. Fortunately!

PG   Would this hijacking therefore be a quality?

JB   I think so.

PG   And would Beaubourg be a case in point?

JB   Instead of being contextual, it has created a vacuum around itself: it's a black body. With its flexible spaces, its non-qualitative, spread-out spaces, its transparency was supposed to be in phase with the modern era and it crashed into a mass which came to opacify all these intentions: it no longer fulfils in any way what was supposed to be its dearest desire. Contradiction played a savage part[2].

PG: Could this reversal be calculated?

JB: You could say to yourself: 'I'm going to bring contradiction into play', that wouldn't prevent an ardent reverse . . . I agree about contradictions and paradoxes but it must be clearly understood that it is still the creator who is trying to take back control of the situation . . .

JN: . . . who is trying to play! Here I'd like to quote a passage from *Fatal Strategies* because there I find exactly what I'm looking for:

> *'We are all players. That is to say that what we hope for most intensely is for rational step-by-step links to be broken from time to time and the unprecedented sequence of another order installed, even briefly. We hope for a marvellous hyperbole of events, an extraordinary succession of the smallest details, as if predestined, giving the impression that things that had previously been held artificially apart by a contract of succession and causality suddenly turn out not to have happened by chance, but spontaneously converge and compete to the same intensity by their very sequence'.*

In many of my projects, you will find the wish to collect together things that ought never to have been brought together, to initiate a poetic game of encounters that are often denounced as the height of bad taste, like for example an encounter between the banks of the Marne and a motorway . . .!

JB: I agree. I do find that there is a sort of echo between us . . . if only because this game is the opposite of eclecticism which can bring everything together, can do anything, and yet is nothing but a low-class degradation of surrealism, a postmodernism that loosely and immorally translates a restraint. It's a Puritanism that won't forego anything from what might have been one day; that fancies itself as playful, but without the fatality of the game! The world of the postmodernists is totally defatalized: the accident they seek is nothing but the result of probabilities and has only statistical value. However, even in cars there are accidents of passion like that of those two cars that crashed into each other on the Northern motorway: one of them was driven by the wife, the other by the husband!

PG: Then what is to be done? In Nogent, for 'the state of things', Jean 'fixes' the accident, like one fixes a charcoal drawing. What will result from it? In Marne-la-Vallée, in the face of general hyperbole, he aims to be as discreet as possible, and it turns out that everything that was planned around it has not transpired or is not yet realized, and that his building has become, as he says himself, an absurd fragment.

JB: So it's a game with unknown rules! [3]

PG: Can't they be changed then?

JB: They change themselves!

PG: In *Fatal Strategies*, you write: '*It is not morality, nor the positive value system of a society that makes it progress, it is its immorality and vice.*' If that much is understood, why not rely on it?

JB: No, whatever you do, you will fall back into immorality, it will always triumph: everything is round in the end. The earth is round and, in the world of imagination, there should also be an inevitable curvature which resists all flattening, all linearity, all programming. So it's impossible to agitate for immorality or perversion, that's one absolute starting point. There remains this provocation (in the good sense of the term) of which Jean often speaks. I contrasted provocation in the bad sense of the term with seduction, recognizing that the latter can hold a sort of predestination. We don't know the rules of seduction, but the game is played and it's not you who decides whether you can take part. Such a provocation would be a planned seduction, it would be to say to oneself 'there is a theatre of seduction and I am coming to play my part in it.' That is a parody of seduction, it is to degrade it, it is a pornography of it. On the contrary, provocation, in the good sense of the term, would be to do everything possible to make something arise without claiming to know the rules of the game nor to be able to control its reversal.

PG: Does that mean to say that the best way to act then is to push things to their limits? [4]

JB: Exactly!

JN: The difference is that you try to go to the limit of certain ideas, certain hypotheses, while I try only to go to the end of the real, to the limit of what is admissible by a certain number of people whose consensus is necessary for building.

JB: That is a constraint in the world of ideas too. The fatal thought cannot be a position of total and radical subversion, because it cannot be extremism of the critical subject. It's the paradox of the object! You talk about a strategy of the subject and this does indeed need to benefit from a sort of complicity. You need consensus for a seduction.

PG: Should the aim be hidden? Koolhaas explains that to build higher and higher, and closer and closer together, New York architects claimed to be solving the congestion to which they themselves were contributing! A congestion they were attached to since it is that alone that allowed them to build their skyscrapers!

JB: The parallel idea is a strategic minimum!

JN: In architecture, there are always two narratives. The most distorted case was that of the *Dick House*, but any construction always reserves a certain surprise because of the non-saids.

JB: This contradiction between the narrative initiated and your intentions is overtaken by a narrative that has no term or no place on the scene, which is obscene. This reversal is nothing to do with architectural engineering, it is the effect of the ill will that is behind all objects.

JN: Could architecture be an increasingly pointless discipline?

JB: It's a utopia to want to save a scene where, almost inevitably, there is no longer any. That makes me think about that talk on 'the end of the world' that was held on 5th Avenue. The initial reaction was to say to oneself 'what a great idea to have chosen New York, it's ideal since it's the epicentre of the end of the world,' then you think 'but it's completely stupid to talk about that here because the end of the world has already happened right here'. Finally, you realized that the reason for this assembly of intellectuals was to save 'the idea' of the end of the world, compared to its banal reality that exists in precisely this place. To save this end-of-world utopia, now there's a job for an intellectual! Perhaps it's the same with architecture? That doesn't rule out this job, that revitalizes it. We are working on utopias that have overtaken us with dual control, with retrospective effect (there's no question of slowing down) to save the idea of them because if that were fully realized, it would be the end!

H TONKA: Jean often says that architecture is the tardiest of arts, the one that crystallises a moment that does not belong to it but which would not exist if architecture didn't 'make' it. Architecture is perhaps also saving the idea of forms, it is perhaps a practice which is about 'monstration' of a moment, a moment that is past . . .

JN: . . . and which uses materials drawn from ancillary or parallel disciplines to set and petrify them!

JB: A mixture of extreme nostalgia and anticipation!

JN: I would also say that it's exposing a form of the real which did not exist before . . .

JB: It shouldn't be forgotten that nowadays everything is made against a backdrop of unrealization, of disappearance. The problem of architecture is to work against a backdrop of spatial deconstruction (in its constructiveness, in its co-ordinates, in its imagination too) caused by traffic and speed. Do we need a minimum of gravity, do we need some machines to slow down, to recreate a certain weight (even an artificial one) which would allow us to find ourselves again despite everything? Faced with this state of pure circulation, of pure deconstruction, one can at least play the game to its end. Nevertheless there still comes a point where this is no longer tenable, where everything vanishes . . . like for the game. It is indeed necessary to use something as a stake to make it intense.

HT: Would you see architecture as a stake?

JB: It injects something, not to stabilize because it crystallizes . . . Beaubourg certainly played this role. It was placed there and it caused the crystallization of a fantastic mass. We are plunged into a biochemical crystalloid milieu that is completely unstable and which only wants to implode. One can't escape from this process but perhaps there is a way to play it rather than to undergo it. It is true that, in my writing, I see no other strategies than that one: to create spaces for areas of implosion and crystallization. One must find strategic points that you can make implode in order to draw energy from it that does not dissipate. It is not a question of controlling a process, but of choosing the spot . . . the material of language is perhaps more mobile, in any case it has the advantage that it can be manipulated by a man alone.

JN: In *Fatal Strategies,* you speak of words that take themselves for things. That's a game I play. With me, words often take themselves for things.[5]

JB: In this bazaar, it must indeed be the word or the material itself that takes itself for a thing. It must take the initiative, and this is where the problem arises when you're a master of works, to get rid of this initiative so that it can be master of the game . . .

PG: Is it possible to make their task easier?

JB: Nowadays these poor words collapse under the tons of interpretation. To take them out should still help crystallization. Even if you are not the director of the last act of the tragedy, you can put in place passions but not significations (what we have done to date is concreting, and see where that got us!)

PG: *'Neither monumentality nor beauty are essential in Pompeii, but the fatal intimacy of things, and the fascination of their instantaneousness as a simulacrum of our own death'.* I quote this passage because for me it evokes the mediatheque project in Nîmes.

JN: It's always a temptation to set a moment!

JB: Because at that moment, you leave the linear. Catastrophe necessarily puts you into the cycle. I have always thought that life has two trajectories: one linear, your history, the sequence of things, progress; the other cyclical, where events return and go full circle. These two planes cannot be reconciled: we live one history and one destiny. It is the same for objects. Pompeii is a cyclical object rather than a timeless one. Timelessness is nothing but the imagination of linear time. We all have these recurring phantasms, that we are sure of finding again later, which is literally catastrophic.

PG: Does that square with the contrast you made between the aleatory and the fatal?

JB: The aleatory is a low-intensity game, an undemanding parody.

JN: Is that where you place postmodernism?

JB: Obviously. For me, it's a degraded form of an eclecticism which only knows how to use all the stronger signs that preceded it. It's siding with the absolute simulacrum: you can set up all the commutations you like, you can play endlessly. Ultimately it's too fundamentalist an attitude in the sense that it assimilates too well the situation as it finds it. The situation must be examined from all sides to find a rule or a secret.

JN: Through my rules of form, I try to give my buildings a profundity such that they pose questions and thereby pull you in more and more deeply. I try to give them this resistance to reading by quite complex rules of the game, by scenarios that I explain from time to time in architecture reviews but which the visitor does not know and doesn't need to know. These make the details harmonize with each other and make their anticipated convergences troubling. These scenarios, these histories are there to be found. Could one say that they keep a space for the secret? In any case, they hold the place and give it a tension.

JB: Apart from what you do, what interests you in architecture?

JN: You will have noticed that I'm not much of a historicist. What I seek is to develop a new attitude in relation to the new materials and new referents of thought available to us. What interests me is all the things that are produced today that couldn't have been produced 20 or 30 years ago. I am very concerned with 'updating my knowledge', and very anxious at the thought of not using the potential of the present.

JB: Obviously I'm with you on that, my work is always on topical areas and not part of the history of ideas. Even if there are words that recur from time to time, they are never referential.

PG: Could I take you back for a moment to this opposition you seem to set up between the aleatory and the fatal? I amused myself in a recent article I wrote by connecting a certain fluctuation that affected architecture recently (where solids tend to dematerialize and empty spaces to fill up) with quantum mechanics. Since the latter relies on probabilist data, if I have understood correctly, it must seem to you equally undemanding?

JB: It corresponds to an attitude that is found everywhere, from biology to human relations, so nowadays it is almost a platitude. No doubt architects nowadays put in place a new geometry like *Monsieur Jourdain* did with prose without knowing it, a prose that would be the fractal as described by Mandelbrot.

HT: Neither a strategy in the fatal, nor in the fractal, yet 'Fractal Strategies' against *Fatal Strategies*!

PG: Is that the choice?

JB: The fractal is nevertheless the extreme avatar of linearity gone mad. Linearity wants to extinguish the fractal and abolish all its depth. There is undoubtedly a fatal that results from extreme simulation, perhaps from extreme fractality and a fatal that results from a total antagonism to fractality. But really, at the end of the day, no choice is possible: we must go right to the limits of the system which is not only the state of things, but also the future state of all things, and at the same time take up the exact opposite position to it.

Truth or Radicality: On the Future of Architecture[6]

Let us start out from space, which is after all the primal scene of architecture, and from the radicality of space, which is the void. Is it necessary, and is it possible, to structure or organize that space in any other way than by indefinite horizontal or vertical extension? In other words, when confronted with the radicality of space, is it possible to invent a truth of architecture?

Is there nothing more to architecture than its reality – its references, procedures, functions and techniques? Or does it exceed all these things and ultimately involve something quite different, which might be its own end or something which would allow it to pass beyond its end? Does architecture continue to exist once it has passed beyond its own reality, beyond its truth, in a kind of radicality, a sort of challenge to space (and not simply a management of space), challenge to this society (and not simply a respect for its constraints and a mirroring of its institutions), challenge to architectural creation itself, and challenge to creative architects or the illusion of their mastery? That is the question.

I would like to examine the issue of architectural illusion in two completely opposing senses of the term: on the one hand, to look at architecture insofar as it generates illusion, including illusions about itself, and, on the other, to look at it insofar as it invents a new illusion of urban space and space in general, another scene which exceeds its own grasp.

Personally, I have always been interested in space, and my interest in so-called 'built' objects has been in all those features which give me back the dizzying sense of space. Hence I've found myself interested in such objects as the Pompidou Centre, the World Trade Center and Biosphere 2 – objects which were not exactly (in my view) architectural marvels. It wasn't their architectural significance which captivated me. The question for me was: what is the truth of these objects which – as is the case with most of our great contemporary architectural objects – seem to have been parachuted in from some other world? If, for example, I consider the truth of a building like the World Trade Center, I see that even in the 1960s architecture was already generating the profile of a society and a period which was hyperreal, if not yet actually computerized, with the twin towers resembling nothing so much as two strips of punched tape. In their twinness we might say today that they were already cloned, and were indeed something like a presentiment of the death of 'the original'. Are they, then, an anticipation of our time? Do architects inhabit not the reality, but the fiction of a society? Do they live in an anticipatory illusion? Or are they quite simply expressing what is already there? It is in this sense that I ask the question 'Is there a truth of architecture?' – by which I mean, is there some supra-sensible intended purpose for architecture and space?

Let us try and see how things stand with this 'creative' illusion, with this 'beyond' of architectural reality. The architect's adventure takes place in a world which is eminently real. He or she is in a very particular situation which is not that of an artist in the traditional sense. Architects are not people who sit poring over blank pages or working at canvases. Working to a precise timetable, to a set budget, and for specified persons, they have an object to produce (though one which is not necessarily specified in advance). They work with a team – and are in a situation in which they are going to be limited, directly or indirectly, by considerations of safety and finance and by their own professional organization. Given this situation, where is the scope for freedom, how can they get beyond these constraints? The problem is one of articulating each project to a prior concept or idea (with a very particular strategy in terms of perception and intuition), which is going to define a place of which they have as yet no clear knowledge. We are in the area of invention here, the area of non-knowledge, in the area of risk, and this can in the end become a place where we do not have total control – where things happen secretly, things which are of the order of fate and the voluntary surrender of control. This is where overt illusion enters the picture, the illusion of a space which is not merely visible, but might be said to be the mental prolongation of what one sees, the basic hypothesis here being that architecture is not what fills up a space, but what generates space. This may be achieved through internal visual 'feedback' effects, through the (mis)appropriation of other elements or spaces, through an almost unconscious conjuring. But it is here that the mind kicks in. Take Japanese gardens. There is always a vanishing point, a point where you can't say whether the garden comes to a stop or carries on. Or, again, Jean Nouvel's attempt, with the projected Tour sans Fin at La Défense outside Paris, to go beyond the logic of Albertian perspective (in other words, to organize all the elements so that they are read in an ascending order of scale and thus generate an awareness of space). Though Nouvel's building disappears into the sky, and, being at the outer reaches of sensory perception, verges upon the immaterial, this is not an architecture which is in any sense virtual (though the building has remained virtual in the sense that it has never been built), but one which knows how to create more than merely what one sees.

We have here a mental space of seduction for the eye and the mind.

If I look at the facade of the Fondation Cartier building, also by Jean Nouvel, then because that facade is larger than the building, I don't know whether I'm seeing through glass to the sky or seeing the sky directly. If I look at a tree through three panes of glass, I never know if I'm seeing through to a real tree or seeing a reflection. And when two trees are by chance standing parallel to a pane of glass, I never know whether there's a second tree or whether that, too, is a reflection. This form of illusion is not gratuitous: by the destabilization of perception, it enables a mental space to be created and a scene to be established – a scenic space – without which buildings would merely be constructions and the city itself would merely be an agglomeration of buildings. It is, indeed, from this loss of the scene, with the concomitant thwarting of the viewer's gaze – and, consequently, from the loss of a whole dramaturgy of illusion and seduction – that our cities suffer, being condemned as they are to the saturation of space by an architecture of (both useful and useless) functions.

The most recent presentation of Issey Miyake designs at the Fondation Cartier was a fine illustration of this *mise en scène*, in which the living transparency of the architectural object gave it an active role in the spectacle. Scene one: the Issey Miyake creations, moving around in the inner space. Then the guests' gallery (the women for the most part already dressed in Issey Miyake clothes), unwitting extras in the same *mise en scène*. Then the building itself, reflecting all this – all of it together, seen from outside, presented as one overall event – so that the exhibition site itself became an exhibited object and in the end made itself invisible.

This capacity to be there and at the same time to be invisible seems to me a fundamental quality. This form of what one might call secret (in)visibility is the most effective counter to the currently hegemonic regime of visibility – that dictatorship of transparency in which everything must make itself visible and interpretable, in which the whole aim is to invest mental and visual space, space which is then no longer a space of seeing, but of showing, of making-seen. The antidote to this is an architecture capable of creating both place and non-place, and retaining the charms of transparency without its dictatorship.

The products of such an architecture are unidentified, unidentifiable objects which are a challenge to the surrounding order and stand in a dual – and potentially 'duelling' – relation with the order of reality.

It is in this sense that we can speak not of their truth, but of their radicality. If this duel does not take place, if architecture has to be the functional and programmatic transcription of the constraints of the social and urban order, then it no longer exists as architecture. A successful object is one which exists beyond its own reality, which creates a dual (and not merely interactive) relation (with its users also), a relation of contradiction, misappropriation and destabilization.

The problem is the same in the register of writing and thought and in the political and social orders. Everywhere, whatever you do, you have no choice of events. You merely have a choice of concepts. But that choice is one we hold on to.

Concepts necessarily come into conflict with contexts, with all the (positive), functional meanings a building or a theory – or anything else – may take on. The concept is something which, in relation to the event as it presents itself, as it is interpreted and over-interpreted by the media and the information system, creates the non-event. To the allegedly 'real' event, it opposes a theoretical and fictional non-event. I can see how this can work with writing. It is much less clear how it works with architecture, but in some architectural objects I sense a kind of extrapolation from another space, another scene, there being here an inspiration running counter to any project or functional constraint. This is the only solution to the impossible exchange between space and the city, a solution which is clearly not to be found in the artificial spaces of freedom created in the city. It brings us to the very question of the destiny of architecture when it aspires to some truth. What happens to the project of truth (by which I mean the determined ambition to fulfil a program, to respond to needs, to be a transformer of social or political situations, with a cultural and pedagogic mission, etc. – in short, everything that goes into the official discourse and relates to the conscious will of the architect himself)? For better or for worse, what one finds is that these programmatic intentions are always hijacked by the very people at whom they were aimed. They are reformulated by the users, by that mass of people whose original – or perverse – response can never be written into the project. There is no 'automatic writing' of social relations or of mass needs, either in politics or in architecture. Here too there is always a duel, and the reaction is unpredictable. The reaction in question is that of a fully fledged participant in the process, a participant who tends most often to be included as a passive element, but does not necessarily play by the rules of the game or respect the rules of dialogue. The masses take over the architectural object in their own way and if the architect has not already been diverted from his programmatic course himself, the users will see to it that the unpredictable final destination of that programme is restored. There is another form of radicality here, though in this case it is an involuntary one.

This is how all the intentions which initially shaped the project of the Pompidou Centre were thwarted by the actual object. That project, which was based on positive perspectives of culture and communication, in the end entirely succumbed to the reality – nay, hyperreality – of the object. Instead of being contextual, it created a void all around it. With its flexible, dispersed spaces and its transparency, it ran up against the action of the masses, who rendered it opaque and misused it as only they can. Contradiction came in here in a sort of spontaneous way, and for the Pompidou Centre the effect was something akin to a destiny. The object, the true object, bears within it a kind of fate and it would doubtless be a mistake to attempt to escape this. This calls into question the control exerted by the creator but it is right that it should: wherever one is tempted to assign a function to a place, everyone else will take it upon themselves to make a non-place of it, to invent another set of rules. This is, in a sense, immoral, but, as we know, societies do not progress by their moralities or their positive value-systems, but by their vices and their immorality. And there must surely be a kind of ineluctable curvature to the imagination, as there is to space, which runs counter to any kind of planning, linearity or programming.

In this situation, the architect himself can play at thwarting his own plans, but he cannot aspire to control the object as event, the symbolic rule being that the player is never greater than the game itself. We are all players, gamblers. In other words, our most fervent hope is that rational sequences of events will unravel every now and again and be replaced, if only for a short time, by an unprecedented sequence of a different order, an extraordinary, apparently pre-destined build-up of events, in which things which have until then been artificially kept apart will suddenly appear not to occur randomly, but to be converging, spontaneously and with equal intensity, by the very fact of their being inter-connected.

Our world would not be bearable without this innate power of *détourne-ment*, this 'strange attraction', this radicality originating elsewhere – originating in the object (for radicality comes now not from the subject, but from the object). And there is something attractive in this for architects themselves: to imagine that the buildings they construct, the spaces they invent are the site of secret, random, unpredictable and, in a sense, poetic behaviour and not merely of official behaviour that can be represented in statistical terms.

Having said this, we are confronted in our contemporary world with quite another dimension. A dimension in which the issues of truth and radicality no longer even arise, because we have already passed into virtuality. And there is here a major danger: the danger that architecture no longer exists, that there is no longer any architecture at all.

There are various ways for architecture not to exist. There is a kind of architecture which goes on, and has gone on for millennia, without any 'architectural' conception. People have designed and built their environments by spontaneous rules, and the spaces generated in this way were not made to be contemplated. They had no value as architecture, nor even, properly speaking, any aesthetic value. Even today, what I like about some cities, particularly American ones, is that you can move around them without any thought of architecture. You can travel through them as though travelling through a desert, without indulging in any fine notions of art, history of art, aesthetics or architecture. They are, admittedly, structured to fulfil a multitude of purposes, but, in the way one comes across them, they resemble pure events, pure objects: they enable us to get back to a primal scene of space. In this sense, this is an architecture which serves as anti-architecture (and we can see from Rem Koolhaas' book *Delirious New York* how Manhattan was initially built up on something which had no architectural pretensions, the Coney Island Amusement Park). In my view, perfect architecture is the kind which covers over its own tracks, architecture in which the space is the thought itself. This goes for art and painting too. There are no finer works than those that cast aside all the trappings of art, the history of art and aesthetics. The same goes for thought: the only truly powerful thought is the kind which casts aside the trappings of meaning, profundity and the history of ideas, the trappings of truth . . .

With the coming of the virtual dimension, we lose that architecture which plays on the visible and the invisible, that symbolic form which plays both with the weight and gravity of things and with their disappearance. Virtual architecture is an architecture which no longer has any secret, which has become a mere operator in the field of visibility, a screen-architecture. It has become, as it were, in every sense of these terms, not the natural, but the artificial intelligence of the city and space (I have nothing against artificial intelligence, except when it claims, with its universal calculation, to absorb all the other forms and reduce mental space to a digital one). In order to assess this danger, which is at the same time the danger of the end of the architectural adventure, I shall take an example from another register which 1 know better: photography.

According to Wilhelm Flusser's hypothesis, the immense majority of current photographic images do not express the photographer's choice or vision, but merely deploy the technical resources of the camera. The equipment is in control, pushing itself to the limits of its potential. The human being is merely the technical operator of the programme. This is what 'the virtual' means: the exhaustion of all the technical potentialities of the machine. You can extend this analysis to computers or to artificial intelligence where thought is mostly a mere combinatorial procedure on the part of the software, the virtual and infinite operation of the machine. In this way, everything which takes the technological route, with its immense possibilities for producing diversity, opens on to an 'automatic writing' of the world and it is the same with architecture, which is now exposed to the full range of its technical possibilities.

This is not simply a matter of materials and building techniques; it is also a question of models. Just as all images are possible using the camera, which asks nothing more than to function, so all architectural forms can be revived out of a virtual stock of forms, arranged either conventionally or in some other way. As a result, architecture no longer refers to a truth or originality of some sort, but to the mere technical availability of forms and materials. The truth that emerges is no longer even the truth of objective conditions. Still less is it the truth of the architect's subjective will. It is quite simply the truth of the technical apparatus and its operation. We may still choose to call this 'architecture', but it is not at all clear that it genuinely is so.

Let us take, for example, the Guggenheim Museum in Bilbao, a virtual object if ever there was one, the prototype of virtual architecture. It was put together on a computer out of optional elements or modules, so that a thousand similar museums could be constructed merely by changing the software or the scale of the calculations. Its very relation to its contents – art works and collections – is entirely virtual. The museum, as surprising in its unstable structure and illogical lines as it is unsurprising – and almost conventional – in its exhibition spaces, merely symbolizes the performance of a machinery, an applied mental technology. Now, admittedly, it is not just any old technology and the object is a marvel, but it is an experimental marvel, comparable to the bio-genetic exploration of the body which will give rise to a whole host of clones and chimeras. The Guggenheim is a spatial chimera, the product of machinations which have gained the upper hand over architectural form itself.

It is, in fact, a 'ready-made'. And under the impact of technology and sophisticated equipment everything is becoming 'ready-made'. All the elements to be combined are there already; they merely have to be rearranged on the stage, like most postmodern forms. Duchamp did this with his bottle-rack, with a real object which he turned into a virtual one merely by displacing it. Today, they do it with computer programs and strings of code, but it's the same thing. They take them as they find them and put them on the architectural stage, where they may possibly become works of art. Now one may ask oneself whether this sort of acting-out of Duchamp's, which consists in transposing any old object into the sphere of art by mere displacement (an aesthetic displacement which puts an end to aesthetics, but which opens up at the same time on to a generalized aestheticization) – this revolution of the 'ready-made', which consists in taking real objects and the real world as a pre-given programme for an automatic and infinite aesthetic operation (since all objects are susceptible of entering into this virtual performance), this radical intervention which took place in the field of art and painting – has its equivalent somewhere in the architectural sphere. Is there a break of a similar kind in the history of architecture? Something like a sudden, stark levelling of the sublime sense of aesthetics, as a result of which everything which follows in the field of art will no longer have the same meaning: everything will occur, so to speak, beyond the end, on the basis of the disappearance of art as such. I should like to ask the same question in relation to architecture: hasn't something occurred in architecture which means that all that has happened since has taken place against a background of the disappearance of architecture as such (as history, as the symbolic configuration of a society)? This hypothesis – the hypothesis of something 'beyond' their discipline – ought to be attractive even to architects. The question arises for politics too: doesn't everything which happens today on the so-called political scene actually take place against a background of the disappearance of the real – its disappearance, in effect, into the virtual? This hypothesis is by no means a dispiriting one: it may be more exciting to see what happens beyond the end than purely and simply to prolong the history of art. It gives an original and exceptional character to everything which can come into being beyond that disappearance. If we accept the disappearance hypothesis, it is still possible for anything whatever to appear. I like the radicalism of this hypothesis because I would like architecture, the architectural object, to remain something exceptional and not to sink into that state which threatens us today on all sides: the virtual reality of architecture.

But we are in that state. Architecture is to a large extent doomed today merely to serve culture and communication. In other words, it is doomed to serve the virtual aestheticization of the whole of society. It functions as a museum of the packaging of a social form known as culture, a museum of the packaging of immaterial needs which have no other definition than their being inscribed in numerous buildings designated for cultural ends. When people are not being turned into museum pieces on the spot (in heritage centres, where they become the virtual extras in their own lives, this too being a form of 'ready-made'), they are siphoned off to the huge, more or less interactive warehousing spaces that are the world's cultural and commercial centres, or to places of transit and circulation which have rightly been described as sites of disappearance (at Osaka in Japan they are already building a Memorial to Twenty-First Century Communications). Today architecture is enslaved to all these functions of circulation, information, communication and culture. There is a gigantic functionalism in all this and it is no longer a functionalism based in a mechanical world of organic needs, a real social relation, but a functionalism of the virtual. In other words, it is a functionalism relating, in the main, to useless functions, in which architecture itself is in danger of becoming a useless function. The danger is that we shall see a world-wide proliferation of an architecture of clones, a proliferation of transparent interactive, mobile, playful buildings, built in the image of the networks and of virtual reality, by way of which an entire society will deck itself out with the empty trappings of culture, communication and the virtual, much as it is already decked out with the empty trappings of politics. Can there be an architecture of real time, an architecture of flows and networks, an architecture of the virtual and the operational, an architecture of absolute visibility and transparency, an architecture of space restored to its indeterminacy in all dimensions? A polymorphous, multi-purpose architecture (an example might be the delightful little museum built in Nice by Kenzo Tange, which has been left empty for several years now – a Museum of the Void, in a sense, but also a craft centre or body-building centre or who knows what else). Most current public buildings, which are often over-sized, give the impression not of space, but of emptiness. And the works or people moving around in them seem like virtual objects themselves, there being no apparent need for their presence. Empty functionality, the functionality of the useless space (the Centro Cultural de Belém in Lisbon, the National Library of France, etc.).

Everything is caught up in this metastasis of culture today, and architecture is not spared. It is very difficult now to distinguish between what remains of that secret register, of that singularity I was speaking of – and I do not think it has completely disappeared because I believe it to be indestructible – and what has passed over into the register of culture, which is itself a mental technology involving the ascendancy of all available models. There are of course urban and geographical constraints upon the architect, constraints imposed by financial pressures and by the commission. But, above all, there are models: the models which are in the contractor's or the client's head and all those, too, which circulate in the architectural journals and in the history of architectural forms themselves. All these models impose a certain number of parameters, which means that what is built in the end is most often a collage of objects representing a compromise solution. The tragedy of contemporary architecture is this endless cloning of the same type of living space the world over, as a function of parameters of functionality, or the cloning of a certain type of typical or picturesque architecture. The end result is an (architectural) object which not only fails to reach beyond its own project, but fails even to reach beyond its own programme.

Might we not say, then, that architecture has lost its shadow, to employ an analogy with Adelbert Chamisso's novella, *Peter Schlemihl*, in which the hero sells his shadow to the devil? Architecture, having become the transparent medium for all the models running through it, might now be in a situation where it can only repeat itself to infinity, or work its way through all the possible variations of a pre-programmed code, that code trotting out its generic stock of conventional forms in some pale imitation of the genetic code?

Take the twin towers of the World Trade Center (and I'm not objecting in any sense to the architectural event they constitute, which I find admirable). One might see the one tower as the other's shadow, its exact replica. But the point is that there no longer is any shadow; the shadow has become a clone. The aspect of otherness, secrecy and mystery, for which the shadow is a metaphor, has disappeared, leaving an identical genetic copy in its stead. Now, loss of a shadow means the disappearance of the sun, without which, as we know, things would merely be what they are. And indeed, in our virtual universe, our universe of clones, our shadowless universe, things are merely what they are. And they are so in innumerable copies, multiplied indefinitely, since the shadow in a sense set bounds upon a being; it marked out its individual limit: it was the shadow which prevented it from reproducing itself to infinity.

But the situation is not, in my view, entirely hopeless. Though architecture is no longer the invention of a world, we may hope for it to be something other than a more or less kitsch repetition of itself, something other than a geological layer of concrete – that new sedimentation of the quaternary period. The field of photography offers the possibility of wresting some exceptional images

from the automatic working of the camera, which has infinite technical potentialities and tends to produce an uncontrollable flow of images. As we know,
'automatic writing' is never truly automatic, and there is always a chance of *hasard
objectif*, a chance that an unforeseeable series of events will occur. In the visual
profusion of images that is currently submerging us, there is still a chance of
recreating the primal, primitive scene of the image. In a sense, any image whatever retains something savage and fantastical, and intuition can recover this
punctum (Barthes), this secret of the image, if it is taken literally. But we have to
want that (literalness); we have to secrete that secret, we have to want to thwart
the general aestheticization and the mental technology of culture which are now
upon us.

And so we may believe that in architecture too, starting out from the
spirit of place, the pleasure of place, and taking account of what are often chance
factors, one can invent other strategies, other dramaturgies. We may believe that,
against this universal cloning of human beings, places and buildings, against this
irruption of universal virtual reality, we can effect what I shall term a poetic transference of situation or a poetic situation of transference – towards a poetic
architecture, a dramatic architecture, a literal architecture, a radical architecture –
which, naturally, we all still dream of.

Truth and transcendent aesthetic value have no place here. Nothing is to
be had from the function, the meaning, the project or the programme. Literalness
is all. An example of this? Take the Pompidou Centre. What does that building
speak of? Art, aesthetics, culture? No, it speaks of circulation, storage and flow,
whether of individuals, objects or signs. And the architecture of the Pompidou
Centre says these things well, says them literally. It is a cultural object, a cultural
memorial to the obscure disaster of culture. The fantastic thing about it – even if
this is involuntary – is that it shows both culture and the fate culture has succumbed
to, and is succumbing to increasingly: the perfusion, superfusion and confusion
of all signs. The same goes for the World Trade Center: the wonder of that building
is that it puts on a fantastic urban show, a marvellous show of verticality, and is,
at the same time, the glaring symbol of the fate the city has succumbed to; it is
the symbol of what the city died of as a historical form. This is what gives such

architecture its power: it is a form of extreme anticipation of a lost object and, at the same time, of retrospective nostalgia for that object.

Here, then, are some fragments of a primal scene of architecture, seen through the imagination of an outsider to the profession. You can interpret them literally and in all senses, as Rimbaud put it, one of the possible senses being that there still exists, beyond any illusion or disillusionment, a future of architecture in which I believe, even if that future of architecture is not necessarily architectural. There is a future of architecture for the simple reason that no one has yet invented the building or architectural object that would put an end to all others, that would put an end to space itself. Nor has anyone yet invented the city which would end all cities or the body of thought which would end all thought. Now, at bottom, this is everyone's dream. So long as it does not become a reality, there is still hope.

Notes

1.   Reprinted by permission from Jean Baudrillard, Interview translated from the French by Sheena Cleland, Wordsmith. All the following notes for this interview were written by Hubert Tonka and translated by Sheena Cleland, Wordsmith.

2.   Is there a programmatic face of architecture – a positive response to positive questions - and is there an enigmatic face? With regard to Beaubourg, can one speak of an object that does not fulfil its destiny? Both a structured object and an object of architecture. The structured object appears at the point where the humanist and democratic programme breaks down. There the objectified object appears and thwarts the foreseeable use of the object. The intentions included in these programmes by their planners and the intentions introduced (positively) by the architect can indeed be denied. The fact remains that such architecture gives up its secret and opens up to the enigma of destiny and other types keep the secret, and remain deprived of destiny. A seductive affair! Is that not the modernity of architecture? I would say modernity up until its detachment from being. The object is perverted by creation.

3.   The object naturally escapes from its creator. The object reverts to something else, to its most simple state; it is delivered. Does not the creator too hijack it, as will the user? Is he not also part of the 'silent majority', the depraved animal of the cities? I have always been surprised by the banal discussions of designers, of the deception that they show in chiaroscuro, delivering a nebulous smoke signal – no smoke without fire – where a lie

is established and the dream dies. Architecture is not military thought, it knows no direct strategy, and when that was used it was cataclysmic (the 'modern city') and devastating. There is no aesthetic strategy. Just like seduction, the goal is not pursued or tracked, it imposes itself as an unavoidable destiny. Architecture and women have a lot in common.

4.   We cannot change the language rules of the module by pronunciation or intonation; we can only play with them with words. These rules will still escape from us and change (of their own accord). The interaction remains a secret, we have no interest in it, we are just chatting! An unspoken language is a dead language, a language that does not know its smallest variables is a dying language. Architecture highlights language; it must decline the rule in order to happen. The question is: what do we hear?

5.   Does not architecture contain the least of things? Are we not prisoners of a functional condition of architecture, to which architecture must respond, forgetting the persistence and versatility of the human spirit? I don't understand how functionality could have been taken seriously . . . it's as if one could imagine painting (the art) without paint (the material), without any sort of media sustaining it!

6.   It is by talking about the subjects furthest from architecture that we can best grasp it, and by evoking other things that we evoke it best. We still have some difficulty in expressing the things closest to us, but there is a depth underlying these difficulties. I have often noticed the keen interest that architect friends take in such writings or discussions, while they are unable to make the connection objectively. This sometimes deceptive inability seems to me a healthy astonishment before the undecipherable enigma of creation. Architecture as a black hole, as anti-matter, as non-obvious fact . . . is that the fatality of architecture when it is an object placed in the social project?

The only lighting was video screens showing images of the whole world, shows going on and cars passing through the tunnel.

THE HOMEOPATHIC DISAPPEARANCE

OF ARCHITECTURE: AN INTERVIEW

WITH JEAN BAUDRILLARD

In the context of the fascination of images, seduction is perhaps the only means of overcoming the brutality of desire – the immediacy of the answer – in order to establish a dialogue based on pauses and silence. This interview attempts to carve possible pathways towards a kind of architecture that still results in being capable of surprising, even if only by disappearing through its own transparency.

Aesthetics and design

Francesco Proto: Do you still believe in an aesthetics of architecture?

Jean Baudrillard: Not being an architect at all, I would not know how to face the problem of architectural planning; I could not make a distinction between the project itself and its realization. I remember that 'planning' as a process was already being discussed in Italy in the 1960s and the 1970s. However, the idea of the 'project' always involves the willingness to assign a purpose to architecture, whether this be social, aesthetic, economic or other. I think that architecture is now in the same situation as all the other creative disciplines: the projection, the dramatic 'pre-visioning' or even the possibility of planning is decreasing since things are less and less foreseeable, less programmable. On the contrary, they are more and more aleatory, more fluid, even if I am not sure what the concept of planning in architecture might mean. Certainly, it must be fundamental. Nevertheless, it should be accepted that I am not part of an architectural culture.

The lost language of seduction

FP: Does it make sense to try to find a language of seduction in architecture? Does an object, as such, seduce whether or not the designer intended it to do so?

JB: I would start from an example. The kind of architecture that I know best – that of Jean Nouvel – can, in the end, be considered as an architecture of seduction. In fact, although this architecture is a project and has a structure, it always succeeds as an object, not only in becoming an event but also in disappearing. From this point of view, it is an object capable of seducing and it does so partly by disappearing. And this strategy, a strategy of absence, effectively belongs to the order of seduction, though, in the end there is not any intention to seduce. For this reason, to me, good architecture is something that is capable of disappearing, of vanishing, and not something that pretends to know how to satisfy the needs of the subject, because these needs are incalculable, especially if we are talking of collective needs and desires. The latter in fact are not only difficult to understand, but also too complicated to manage. Certainly, one can always put one's mark on something, so as to impose one's mark on a design. However, this design need not necessarily be interactive. I do not believe in interactive architecture, but in seduction, that is, in a dual relationship. In this case, the object must get into the game, even the architectural one, and when it does, the one who stands in front of it starts getting involved and plays with it. Nevertheless, one does not play in order to have the chance to win, but to enjoy, since one is not in front of a mere functional design.

Success in architecture

FP: Do you think it possible to predict success in architecture?

JB: I am quite sure that success is unpredictable – the Pompidou Centre, in France, can provide an example. It is impossible to predict the response of the consumer. It might happen that they either oppose it or pervert it, just as happened to the Pompidou Centre, where the finality of both culture and communication has been annihilated. Because of the masses it has become a dreadful object of manipulation. It was they who have manipulated it, though the centre was too ambiguous an object to work.

However, there is a new meaning of seduction within a kind of architecture capable of being combinatorial and mobile, and with which it is possible to play just as it was with a new technology. For example, the Guggenheim Museum in Bilbao: as an architectural object made in modules – and it would be possible to build ten new museums with the same elements – it gives the viewer the possibility of playing. On the other hand, it also is a changing object, an object that has the potential to change. Anyone can interact with it in whatever way they want.

Nevertheless, to me it is not an architectural object: it is rather a second or third stage of postmodernism. It is a kind of architecture that uses all the possibilities, all the tools, all the most modern methods by which architecture is now created. But for me, it is not a pure object: it is a combinatory, arbitrary object – just that – but not a pure object.

Duchamp in architecture

FP: Do we have a Duchamp in architecture? Will we ever have one?

JB: I have already asked this question, during the conversations with Jean Nouvel: whether in architecture an event such as Duchamp in art had occurred which would result in the end of architecture as an aesthetic. From Duchamp on, paintings or art have not been and never will be the same again. I cannot say whether a Duchamp in architecture has occurred, maybe architects should know. However, at first sight, I have not got the impression of a change. What might have happened is difficult to say, because in this field one cannot move an object, subtract it from its aesthetic context and, all of a sudden, destroy it. It cannot be done in architecture since it still has a useful, instrumental function. For this reason, I cannot imagine a Duchamp in architecture. Nevertheless, I am convinced that in some way, it has happened . . . slowly, in homeopathic doses. We can see that Duchamp, in the end, is the disappearance of art. Later, yes, something has survived, but always on the basis of the disappearance of art as aesthetics. To some extent, I also believe that architecture should be seen on the basis of the disappearance of architecture as we know it. This way, we would not have a conventional, functional discipline, especially with the Guggenheim, which represents the ideal moment in architecture: its definition, its algebra, the highest point in contemporary architecture. Beyond this point, we have only witnessed a change, a disappearance.

In art, we have the same effect as with Duchamp but, as far as I know, there is no single and precise event that might have determined such a change, though I think it has occurred. What should be done in architecture afterwards, is the same problem as what has been done in art: one can use the same elements, though with a different meaning. They have not got the same symbolic value as before. In fact, architecture is not any longer the expression of the symbolic shape of a society; nowadays, it can be a décor, or a game, but it does not represent the structure of a town. This is now done using urban or engineering strategies.

Nowadays, architecture – at least the kind of architecture that keeps on being noticed – is made of objects. Yes, because the other one – the 'architectural architecture' – is not subjected to collective responsibility any longer. There are creations, objects that seem to be without links one to the other. They have a style, but it cannot be said that one of them can qualify an age or a society. According to my way of thinking, it is just this that has disappeared: the symbolic. Because there are no values left, there are no important collective values to be expressed in terms of space. And space itself has been secularized, vulgarized, so that there are fewer and fewer symbolic pathways.

The object as a sign

FP: If attention precedes seduction, how can an architectural object, considered as a sign, emerge among the pre-existing signs of the town?

JB: Today we live in a world of advertisements, when even architecture builds itself on an advertising model and, for this reason most of all, attracts attention. Later, to seduce, it must become a proper sign. However, nowadays, it is just like all the other advertising signs: they are signals, therefore they have to attract attention. Then, they may either work or not and there is an entire strategy for that. But seduction is something else. It is necessary that the sign itself becomes a 'sign', constitutes itself as something special in order to become an accomplice and help the viewer to read it as something exceptional. All the signs that can be found in the city, the advertising signals, are not accomplices: we see them, we read them but, once deciphered, they just create automatism and nothing else. The true sign – to give back to the word its own nobility – is something else. It is an extraordinary event: this way, the sign becomes and assumes a particular meaning. This is seduction, and is something very different from attention. Unfortunately, today, in our urban signals, the two things become confused in a kind of amalgam of manipulation. Architecture has in part escaped from this mechanism, at least I hope so – but it has also become for the most part 'advertised'. It has renounced becoming a pure object of seduction to become not only a functional object, a thing that, in one way or another, it has always been, but also to have, most of all, an advertised existence, to be fashionable. Often, objects from great designers – therefore the signed objects – are recognizable simply from the sign being identically repeated from one object to another. And this is a way to let the object show itself: to make it visible, as is typical in advertising. At this point, audience and advertiser should be differentiated, in order to understand whether these objects can be considered as public ones. They should still hold a symbolic and collective function and therefore mean something for the community.

This is difficult to predict because it is the masses themselves who create the meaning of something – in the end, the meaning as such does not exist, it is the one who receives it that creates her/his own meaning. But the masses are massive, neutral and impersonal, and will not succeed in creating any meaning;

on the contrary, they will destroy it. And the object, in the middle, will have to protect itself. Certainly, the game is not a simple one, but the die is cast, and architects will always have to fight against the masses' indifference towards the object.

Space as a thought

FP: What do you mean when you say that 'perfect architecture' occurs when 'space results in being the thought itself'?

JB: We have already talked about it: it is the object that disappears, it is the strategy of disappearance itself or, at least, the strategy of the secret, the place where the secret lies. In contrast to the advertising we were talking about, we need to find the secret. For the advertiser, used to being linked to the sign and to the code of signals, the secret is connected to the footprint, which is something that can be erased.

My idea is that architecture starts from space, which is the primary scene, and that architecture fills it; but it is the empty space that should increase the symbolism in architecture. Architecture should anyway always manage to hold this emptiness, to be somewhere inside it, in the sense that it should not always be a 'full' architecture, a functional one, a space-destroyer. At that point, instead of space, what we are left with is a kind of functional dimension, whereas architecture must keep on belonging to the empty space. This empty space does not have to exist in the physical dimension. It can also exist in the mental one. Architecture should embody a sort of empty nucleus, an empty matrix of interior space, in order to be capable of generating a space instead of managing it.

However, there is a further distinction between a kind of architecture that produces space and another that manages it. Both of them should avoid filling it in order not to destroy it.

BAUDRILLARD, PERSPECTIVE

AND THE VOID OF ARCHITECTURE

KEITH BROADFOOT AND REX BUTLER

Towards the end of the interview with Francesco Proto, Baudrillard says the following about architecture:

> My idea is that architecture starts from space, which is the primary scene, and that architecture fills it . . . Architecture should anyway always manage to hold this emptiness, to be somewhere inside it, in the sense that it should not always be a 'full architecture', a functional one, a space-destroyer . . . Architecture should embody a sort of empty nucleus, an empty matrix of interior space, in order to be capable of generating a space instead of managing it.[1]

How are we to understand the distinction Baudrillard is making here between these two types of architecture? What is the difference between an architecture that 'destroys'' space and an architecture that 'creates' space, between an architecture that is 'full' and an architecture that is 'empty'? What is the nature of that void or emptiness in terms of which Baudrillard sees architecture in its 'primary' or original state? And what happens to this emptiness once architecture enters the 'functional' realm? How does it allow architecture to 'generate' space and not to 'manage' it?

In fact, with these remarks Baudrillard places himself within a long line of thinkers who have suggested that architecture ultimately concerns something other than space. Without going back too far, it is striking, for instance, how Baudrillard's ideas intersect with those of Lacan. For Lacan too there is the same concern to connect architecture to an emptiness or void. We find a similar sugges- tion that architecture should embody a vacant nucleus or core. More precisely, in Lacan – and we will see the relationship with Baudrillard in a moment – it is a matter of architecture 'rediscovering' this emptiness at a moment when it most resembles painting, or painting most resembles architecture. As he says: 'Since it is a matter of finding once more the sacred void of architecture in the less marked medium of painting, the attempt is made to create something that resembles it more and more closely, that is to say, perspective is discovered'.[2]

And, again, as with Baudrillard, Lacan emphasizes that it is not a matter of architecture simply fitting into a pre-existing space, filling it up in a match with it, but on the contrary of creating a certain void or lack, an absence or emptiness that can never entirely be made up. It is into this emptiness that Lacan places *das Ding* in his well-known analysis of the vase, which introduces both emptiness and fullness into a world that had not 'previously known of them'.[3] But for Lacan this void, what Baudrillard refers to as 'radicality' of architecture is always lost, covered over or given only in the guise of something else. It is from the beginning missing or displaced, allowing other things to signify around it, bringing about 'empti- ness' and 'fullness' and even the exchange between them. This is why Baudrillard too will speak of that emptiness which lies at the origin as a kind of 'lost object', which can never be grasped as such but conceived only in the mode either of 'extreme anticipation' or 'retrospective nostalgia'.[4]

A crucial moment in the thinking of all of this for both Baudrillard and Lacan is the appearance of perspective. For Lacan, as we have seen, perspective is that which allows the passing over of painting into architecture in the finding once more – which also means the losing once more – of the sacred void. And perspective is decisive also to Baudrillard's understanding of architecture. We can indeed trace Baudrillard's more recent pronouncements on architecture back to a much earlier essay on *trompe l'oeil*, which originally appeared in the book *On Seduction* in 1979. In this essay, we find the distinction between 'space-destroying' and 'space-creating' architecture being played out in terms of that between perspectival and *trompe l'oeil* painting. Perspective is an art of simulation and fullness, while *trompe l'oeil* is an art of seduction and emptiness. In *trompe l'oeil*, we get a glimpse – as though seeing for a moment the 'wrong' or 'reverse' side of things – of what allows the simulated space of perspective. *Trompe l'oeil* does not merely abolish or render inoperative perspective, but rather, as Baudrillard says, exposes it as a 'principle', reveals that void for which it stands in and which makes it possible.[5]

However, the real significance of *trompe l'oeil* within perspective might be better explained by reference to the first historical 'discovery' of perspective by Filippo Brunelleschi in 1425. What Brunelleschi produces in his famous optical device in which he looks out at a reflection of a painting in a mirror through a small hole drilled in the back of that painting is in fact a perfect model of simulation. By means of the 'effect of the real' thereby created, it is as though the spectator coming to the painting was actually looking at the Church of San Giovanni in Florence from the same point of view inside the Church of Santa Maria del Fiore from which Brunelleschi painted it. There is henceforth a radical doubling or confusion between reality and fiction, between an architecture that is a painting and a painting that is an architecture. From this moment on, as Baudrillard says of simulation, we can no longer tell which comes first or what is being modelled on what.

But again for Baudrillard what is crucial here in this inaugural moment of perspective is the role of the void. It is created by Brunelleschi's original act of drilling a hole in the back of the painting (which is also to create a void within the architectural space of the church); but at the same time as it is created, it is also removed or covered over. It exists, as Baudrillard says, only as a 'lost' object, which is lost as soon as it is found or is lost in being found. In the Brunelleschi optical device, that is, in order to enter the perspectival space the spectator's eye

must cover over or take the place of the void at the back of the painting; it literally has to become blind to this void (it cannot see itself reflected in the mirror
held opposite). To recall for a moment Baudrillard's distinction between 'space-
destroying' and 'space-creating' architecture, this void does not merely fit within
an already existing space but comes before it, opening up the very emptiness and
fullness of perspectival space itself. And yet within this space it is invisible; to
take up the etymological meaning of the word 'perspective', it is what we look
through (*per-specare*) in order to see this space at all. However, at certain rare
moments, as Baudrillard suggests, we are able within this space to glimpse this
void, somehow to retrace or return to its origin. Baudrillard's privileged example
of this is *trompe l'oeil*, but this return is repeated throughout the history of art
and architecture, insofar as with simulation it is not a matter of its historical development but of it being suddenly there all at once only because something is missing
from it something that will forever withhold the seductive power of the secret.

In order to see how all of this might apply to modern architecture, we
might remind ourselves of Baudrillard's comments on Frank Gehry's Guggenheim
Museum at Bilbao. He says that it constitutes a kind of architectural readymade,
in that what we have in it is a simple transposition of pre-existing 'computer programs and strings of code' from a virtual mental space to a physical real space.[6]
And indeed the effect of museums like this is to turn the art within them also into
readymades, for at once – and Baudrillard is following here an analysis by Walter
Benjamin – anything within its empty space appears special and the work's value
no longer appears in itself but only in its symbolic or aesthetic framing by the
institution. That is to say, like the readymade, the art objects in these new museums
are rendered unique by their placement within them, and yet for the same reason
they become substitutable for any number of others. In a way, we cannot help thinking of the reflective titanium surface of Bilbao as equivalent to the burnished silver
of Brunelleschi's optical device, for we have here the same folding over of illusion onto reality and art onto architecture. And the same analysis applies to the
Pompidou Centre. In the building's radical externalization of its inside, there is
exactly the same confusion of art and architecture, so that we can no longer tell
what is inside and what is outside the museum. The rubbish in the streets outside

the museum seems part of the exhibition inside, while the art inside resembles the rubbish in the streets. The result, says Baudrillard, is at the same time a generalized aestheticization of reality and the end of aesthetics, in other words, the highest stage of simulation.[7]

The distinction we might make between these 'monstrosities' and, say, Jean Nouvel's unbuilt project for Tête Défense, which Baudrillard calls a 'successful architectural object',[8] might initially appear very slight. Tête Défense is a project in which, by building skyscrapers on either side of a long sight-line in Haussmannian Paris, Nouvel hoped as it were to frame the sun as it rose above and fell beneath the horizon at morning or night. As the sun approaches the skyscrapers it is intended to render them transparent, causing them to disappear, leaving behind only their shadows. Now at first sight nothing could appear more like a readymade, with the aesthetic framing of reality by these skyscrapers rising up on either side of the sun, or indeed like a simple remake of Brunelleschi in its attempt to turn the sky into the background of a painting. Nouvel, however, in his various interviews on the project insists that it is a conscious attempt to go beyond what he calls 'Albertian' perspective, in which the sky is always an 'unfinished canvas':

> Certainly there is at first the effect of an absolutely perfect
> perspective, but as soon as one approaches it, one has the
> impression of a badly printed drawing; one sees precisely the
> out-of-focus nature, the vagueness with which it is created. It is in
> total contradiction with the classical means of placing a building
> within a perspective, properly situated beneath the horizon as an
> object that detaches itself, as an object that imposes itself. What
> interests me is the idea of a *continuum*, of erasing the limits, of
> exploring the profound nature of atmosphere.[9]

Indeed, in an almost uncanny way, Nouvel's description here repeats almost word for word Baudrillard's account of *trompe l'oeil*. Strangely enough, because, after all, Nouvel uses a real sun in his work, looking at these crystalline

buildings pierced by the sun's rays on either side of Tête Défense, we might think
of Baudrillard's notion that '*trompe l'oeil* functions in weightlessness, as indicated
by the vertical backdrop, everything being suspended, the object, time, even light
and perspective. While the still life still uses classic shape and shade, the shadows
borne by the *trompe l'oeil* lack the depth that comes from a real luminous
source'.[10] Or, along the lines of Nouvel's desire to erase the limits between the
building and the world, we can read: 'A different universe occupies the foreground
[of *trompe l'oeil*], a universe without horizon or horizontality, like an opaque
mirror placed before the eye, with nothing behind it'.[11] Perhaps most importantly,
like trompe l'oeil and unlike the readymade, what Nouvel aims at in his work is
not the indirect representation but the direct *presentation* of things: it is not an
image or a reflection of the sun or sky we see, as in Brunelleschi, but the sun and
sky themselves. That aesthetic framing of reality that we find in contemporary
museums disappears – it is just this disappearance of architecture that Baudrillard
approves of in Nouvel – so that we no longer have an essentially vicarious object
elevated by virtue of its placement into a position of singularity.

Instead – and this is what Baudrillard means by *trompe l'oeil* exposing
perspective as a 'principle' – what Nouvel wants to gesture towards is the moment
'preceding' this, that void which allows the exchange between illusion and reality,
the one and the many. And he does this by *reversing* the set up of Brunelleschi's
optical device in Tête Défense, so that we appear to be looking out from behind
the surface of things, identifying us not with the gaze that looks onto the object
or the light that illuminates the world but with the object being looked onto by the
gaze (that of the sun itself), illuminated ourselves as part of the picture. It is almost
as though in Tête Défense Nouvel has realized an earlier fantasy Baudrillard had
when walking through Le Parc de la Villette: 'Why not build a giant *camera
obscura*, where we can pass to the other side of the lens (through which we are
seen, through which the object sees us), or indeed a gigantic hologram, through
which we can pass into the light?'[12] In that subtle shift of 'focus' or 'vagueness'
that Nouvel speaks of, like that sudden 'break with reality' that Baudrillard says
is at stake in *trompe l'oeil*, in seeing the work from the other side as the sun moves
across the buildings making two dimensional objects three dimensional it is as

though we were actually witnessing that original exchange between illusion and reality and painting and architecture for the first time. But it is a process that repeats itself every morning or evening, just as this showing of the void at the origin of art is implicit in every work of art. It is no sooner revealed than covered over, which is why the history of art is nothing more than the incessant return to this lost origin, a cycle itself like the rise and fall of the sun.

Notes

1. 'The Homeopathic Disappearance of Architecture: An Interview with Jean Baudrillard', see p 175
2. Jacques Lacan, *The Ethics of Psychoanalysis*, Tavistock, London, 1992, p 136
3. Ibid, p 120
4. See p 172
5. See p 90
6. See p 167
7. See p 29
8. See p 23
9. Jean Nouvel, 'Espèces d'espace', in Baudrillard (ed. François L'Yvonnet), Éditions de l'Herne, Paris, 2004, p 181
10. See pp 88–89
11. See p 90
12. See p 71. Of course, in another way, Nouvel has also realized his fantasy with his Institut du Monde Arabe. His plan for Tours sans Fin would also be interesting to think of in the context of this 'anamorphosis' of space and the desire of architecture to turn around endlessly to witness its own origin – the other meaning of 'tours sans fin'.

Keith Broadfoot teaches in the Department of Art History and Theory at the University of Sydney.

Rex Butler teaches in the School of English, Media Studies and Art History at the University of Queensland.

ESSENTIAL BIBLIOGRAPHY

In brackets, publication date of the original French edition.

1997, *The System of the Objects*. Translated by James Benedict. London/New York: Verso (1968).

1998, *The Consumer Society: Myth and Structures*. London: Sage (1970).

1981, *For a Critique of the Political Economy of the Sign*. Translated by Charles Levin. US: Telos (1972).

1998, *Symbolic Exchange and Death*. Translated by Iain Hamilton Grant. London: Sage (1976).

1990, *Seduction*. Translated by B. Singer. London: Macmillan (1979).

1994, *Simulacra and Simulations*. Translated by Paul Foss, Paul Patton and Philip Beitchman. Ann Arbor: University of Michigan Press (1981).

1990, *Fatal Strategies*. Translated by Philip Beitchman. London: Semiotext(e)/Pluto (1983).

1988, *America*. Translated by Chris Turner. London/New York: Verso (1986).

1987, *The Ecstasy of Communication*. Edited by Sylvère Lotringer and translated by Bernard and Caroline Schutze. New York: Semiotext(e) (1987).

1990, *Cool Memories [1980–1985]*. Translated by Chris Turner. London/New York: Verso (1987).

1997, *Cool Memories II [1987–90]*. London/New York: Verso (1990).

1997, *Fragments: Cool Memories III [1990–95]*. Translated by Emile Agar. London/New York: Verso (1995).

2003, *Cool Memories IV [1995–2000]*. Translated by Chris Turner. London: Verso (2000).

1995, *The Gulf War Did Not Take Place*. Translated by Paul Patton. Sydney: Power (1991).

1994, *The Illusion of The End*. Translated by Chris Turner. Cambridge: Polity (1992).

1996, *The Perfect Crime*. Translated by Chris Turner. London/New York: Verso (1995).

2003, *Passwords*. Translated by Chris Turner. London: Verso (2000).

FURTHER READING

Baudrillard, Jean, *The Spirit of Terrorism,* London: Verso, 2003.

Baudrillard, Jean, and Jean Nouvel, *The Singular Objects of Architecture*. Robert Bononno (Trans). London/Minneapolis: University of Minnesota Press, 2002.

Codeluppi, Vanni, *La Società pubblicitaria: Consumo, Mass Media, Ipermodernità* [The Advertising Society: Consumption, Mass Media, Hypermodernity]. Genoa: Costa & Nolan, 1996.

Amendola, Giandomenico, *La Città Postmoderna* [The Postmodern City], Bari: Laterza, 1997.

Leach, Neil, *The Anesthetics of Architecture*, Cambridge, Mass: MIT Press, 1999.

Augé, Marc, *Impossible voyage: le tourisme et ses images*, Paris: Payot & Rivages, 1997

Crossing n°1, 'Media Building', monographic issue, Dec 2000.

Hale, Jonathan, *Building Ideas: An Introduction to Architectural Theory*, Chichester: Wiley, 2000.

Masiero, Roberto, *Estetica dell'Architettura* [The Aesthetics of Architecture], Bologna: Il Mulino, 1999.

Fjellman, Stephen M, *Vinyl Leaves: Walt Disney World and America*, Boulder: Westview Press, 1992.

Prestinenza Puglisi, Luigi, *Hyperarchitecture*, Berlin: Birkhauser, 1999.

Gane, Mike, *Baudrillard's Bestiary,* London: Routledge, 1991.

Genosko, Gary, *The Uncollected Baudrillard*, London: Sage, 2001.

Butler, Rex, *Jean Baudrillard: The Defence of the Real*, London: Sage, 1999.

Silver, Nathan, *The Making of the Beaubourg*, MIT Press, 1997.